The Welsh Dockers

The Welsh Dockers

Philip J. Leng

G. W. & A. Hesketh, Ormskirk

First published 1981 by G. W. & A. Hesketh, P.O. Box 8, Aughton Street,
Ormskirk, Lancashire L39 5HH, Great Britain,
and at 18765 Tuba Street, Northridge, California 91324, U.S.A.

Copyright © Philip J. Leng, 1981.
Design by G. W. & A. Hesketh, Ormskirk, L39 5HH.
Printed in Great Britain by Bridgeman Westall, Sefton Industrial Estate,
Maghull, Merseyside.

ISBN 0 905777 08 5 Paperback.

To my wife and parents

Contents

Contents

Tables

Plates

1. They came to the opening of the New Tredegar Arms, Newport *(by courtesy of Polypill, Newport)*.

2. This is a view of the Old Town Dock, Newport, opened in 1842. It is from a drawing by J.F. Mullock (1818-92), and seems to have been made about the middle of the century *(by courtesy of Newport Museum and Art Gallery)*.

3. The Bute East Dock, Cardiff, during the 1890's: a view taken from the dock entrance looking north, and showing a ship being loaded at the coal tips *(by courtesy of South Glamorgan Libraries, Cardiff)*.

4. A pit-head scene in a South Wales valley *(by courtesy of the National Museum of Wales)*.

5. The coal tips at the Queen Alexandra Docks, Cardiff, in 1907. Cory Brothers were coalowners, and major exporters at the port *(by courtesy of South Glamorgan Libraries, Cardiff)*.

6. Loading patent fuel on the South Wales waterfront *(by courtesy of the National Museum of Wales)*.

7. Unloading pitwood at Barry Docks in c. 1911. Dockers on shore who carried the wood across the railway track and piled it in stacks were paid approximately eight shillings a day *(by courtesy of the National Museum of Wales)*.

8. A warning to strikers. The Bute Docks Company posted this notice concerning the conditions of employment during the Cardiff coal tippers dispute of 1891 *(by courtesy of South Glamorgan Libraries, Cardiff)*.

9. Two opponents of the Dockers' Union: **a.** Sir William Thomas Lewis *(by courtesy of the National Museum of Wales)* and **b.** Mr. Frank Houlder *(by courtesy of Mr. John M. Houlder, C.B.E)*.

10. J. Havelock Wilson, leader of the Seamen's Union, leaving the Law Courts, Cardiff, in July 1911 following the release of Captain Edward Tupper *(by courtesy of South Glamorgan Libraries, Cardiff)*.

11. Tupper on a balcony in Bute Street, Cardiff, addresses dockers and seamen during the 1911 dock strike *(by courtesy of South Glamorgan Libraries, Cardiff)*.

12. Blacklegs at work. Edward England's clerks unloading potatoes during the 1911 dock strike at Cardiff *(by courtesy of South Glamorgan Libraries, Cardiff)*.

13. Out in sympathy! Cardiff coal trimmers leave their work at the docks and march through the city in support of the dockers' pay claim of 1911 *(by courtesy of South Glamorgan Libraries, Cardiff)*.

Preface

This book is concerned with the development of the Dock, Wharf, Riverside and General Labourers' Union in South Wales from its formation in London in 1889 until its amalgamation with other organisations in 1922 to form the Transport and General Workers' Union. It attempts to outline the union's aims and to explain the factors influencing its progress. The union was also prominent in other districts at various times, but South Wales has been concentrated upon because the union always had important strongholds there; because of the wide range of commodities handled at the ports of the Principality; because the attitude of employers on these waterfronts differed so significantly; and because Dockers' officials also recruited workers from other industries in the area.

The union's development has been divided into four sections: its early expansion at the ports and subsequent defeats by employers; its survival on the waterfront between 1894 and 1910, and its recruitment of tinplate workers; its expansion between 1911 and 1914; its growth during the First World War and development until the formation of the T.G.W.U. An introductory section provides a brief description of the growth of the ports of South Wales during the nineteenth century and outlines their trade. In addition, it examines the system of employment on the waterfront and the characteristics of the labour force engaged, for these influenced considerably the structure of the Dockers' Union and its policies.

I became interested in this subject largely because members of my family contributed to the history of waterfront trade unionism in South Wales. My great grandfather, Frank Berry, was an early member of the Dockers' coal trimmers' branch in Newport, and four of his sons followed his footsteps as coal trimmers and as members of the union. Furthermore, my grandfather, Frank Kendall, after leaving Cornwall and working as a railway navvy in Somerset and the South Wales valleys, spent the rest of his working life at Newport docks. He became Chairman of the Dockers' general cargo workers' branch in 1920, and was a close friend of Alfred Cox who also features prominently in this story. I am extremely grateful to my grandfather for spending much time explaining to me conditions and labour relations on the South Wales waterfront.

I also wish to thank Dr. B. J. Atkinson of Eliot College, The University of Kent at Canterbury, for his considerable help and encouragement during the research and writing of this book. Moreover, a large number of archivists, research officers and librarians have given me great assistance. In particular, I have been aided by Mr. W. R. Lucas and the staff of Newport Museum and Reference Library, Mr. H. McKenzie of the National Museum of Wales, Mr. R. Padfield of Cardiff Central Library, Mr. D. Bevan of University College of Swansea, the Transport and General Workers' Union, the Trades Union Congress, the British Historical Transport Records Office, the British

Museum Newspaper Library at Colindale, and the London School of Economics. Finally, I am indebted to my wife, Christine, for her great support and for typing my work. I shall always be grateful to her.

Philip J. Leng
Tunbridge Wells, 1980

Introduction

The ports of South Wales during the nineteenth century: their development, trade and labour force.

In the eighteenth and nineteenth centuries the "Industrial Revolution" affected many parts of Great Britain. New techniques led to an expansion of the iron, coal and cotton industries, large centres of population developed, and improvements in transportation occurred. In South Wales and Monmouthshire the valleys and estuaries in particular were exploited by industry. Copper, iron and tinplate works were established, pits were sunk, and villages grew into towns. Canals and railways were also built, and made it more practicable for the masters of industry to send their products to the coast.

In South Wales the copper industry was established in the Swansea district by 1750 and remained concentrated there throughout the nineteenth century. It was situated in this area because the coals of West Wales suited the smelting of non-ferreous materials, and because an abundant supply of ore was obtained from Cornwall and was easily transported along navigable rivers to the smelting works. After 1750 the iron industry also became prominent, especially in Monmouthshire and north Glamorgan where local supplies of coal, iron-ore and limestone were available. By the early 1820's many iron works were in operation, and they were connected to the coast by canals which were opened for traffic during the 1790's. These works also supplied the tinplate industry which was largely concentrated in the eastern valleys until 1850, when it became increasingly prominent in West Wales.

Along with the growth of these industries, the coal industry in South Wales expanded after 1750. It chiefly supplied local works. Although coal was transported from tidal harbours at Cardiff, Swansea, Llanelly and Newport, the total quantity of coal shipped from the Principality in 1799 was less than 325,000 tons. By the late 1830's, though, the shipment of coal increased considerably (see Table 1), the demands of the Cornish copper mines for semi-anthracite coal grew, and bituminous coal was distributed to many British towns for domestic purposes. The extension of these trades led to the construction of docks at the Welsh ports.

Coal entering Newport and Cardiff for shipment between 1835 and 1840.[1]

	Newport	Cardiff
1835	499,096 (tons)	176,374 (tons)
1836	487,076	192,241
1837	517,066	226,671
1838	497,374	189,081
1839	518,916	211,214
1840	558,104	248,484

Table 1

Docks were also established in South Wales because of the growth of the pig-iron trade. After 1820 many firms became involved in activities such as shipbuilding and the manufacture of cables, and obtained large quantities of metal from the Welsh iron furnaces. The output of pig-iron in South Wales was further advanced considerably by the growth of the railways.

Iron entering Newport and Cardiff for shipment between 1835 and 1839.[2]

	Newport	Cardiff
1835	153,085 (tons)	114,936 (tons)
1836	149,590	115,923
1837	142,108	124,810
1838	166,722	130,637
1839	174,803	132,781

Table 2

As a result of these developments, communications and port facilities were improved. By the early 1840's five docks were constructed, the largest of which were opened at Cardiff in 1839 and Newport in 1842. In 1841 the Taff Vale Railway was also opened, and provided an important connection between Merthyr and Cardiff.

Following the improvements of these ports, pig-iron and bituminous coal exports increased further. Shipments of semi-anthracite coal and metallurgical products also grew at Llanelly and Pembrey where docks were opened in 1836. At Swansea, however, coal and metal exports did not increase so significantly because rival landowners held up the construction of docks. A floating harbour was completed there in 1851, but the first dock was not opened until 1859. Neath also experienced this difficulty: a dock at Briton Ferry which could serve the Neath Valley was not built until 1860.

A large proportion of the capital required for the improvement of waterfront facilities in South Wales was invested by wealthy landlords. At Cardiff the Second Marquis of Bute, the owner of much urban and mineral land in Glamorgan, financed the Bute West Dock which was completed in 1839; at Newport Sir Charles Morgan, a prominent Monmouthshire landowner, backed the construction of the Town Dock three years later. These affluent individuals attempted to set up profitable enterprises and at the same time to establish outlets for their rich mineral possessions in the valleys of Glamorgan and Gwent. At Swansea, on the other hand, less interest was shown towards the development of docks by the West Walian landlord, the Duke of Beaufort. Yet this was not the only difference which existed between the three principal ports of the country. Whereas Cardiff and Newport docks were controlled by private companies, the port of Swansea was administered by a Harbour Trust which had been set up by an Act of Parliament of 1791 to

4

improve and enlarge the harbour of Swansea. Its constitution was framed by the Corporation, but was subsequently amended by the Trustees themselves. Membership of the Trust, according to the constitution of 1879, included the Duke of Beaufort and another landlord, the Earl of Jersey, local shipping and industrial interests, and the representatives of the burgesses of the borough.

Prosperous landowners continued to support the provision of docks in South Wales after 1850, but colliery proprietors and industrial magnates also became involved with the improvement of port facilities. As they wanted to increase their exports, they financed new companies which built large docks. In 1865 the Taff Vale Railway Company leased a dock at Penarth which originated from a scheme devised by wealthy coal owners such as Crawshaw Bailly; and at Newport Sir Charles Morgan and Sir George Elliot, a director of the Powell-Duffryn Coal Company, established the Alexandra Dock Company and backed the construction of the Alexandra North Dock in 1875. At Cardiff, however, developments continued to be financed by the Bute family. Even though the Bute Docks Company was formed in 1887 to manage affairs at the port, it remained reliant upon the vast resources of the Marquis of Bute.

Before the change of management in 1887, the Bute family made a number of important improvements at Cardiff such as the Bute East Dock and the Roath Basin which were completed in 1859 and 1874. Nevertheless, insufficient accommodation for shipping was available at the port during the 1880's, and local freighters became very dissatisfied with the congestion of the waterfront and the high dock charges imposed. As a result a group of colliery owners and coal shippers obtained Parliamentary powers to open a new dock at Barry in 1889. Their venture was very successful. In spite of the construction of the Prince of Wales Dock at Swansea in 1881, the Roath Dock at Cardiff in 1887, the South Dock at Newport in 1892, and the New Dock at Port Talbot in 1898, Barry obtained much trade. Coal shipments at the port increased rapidly and surpassed by 1913 the annual coal exports of Cardiff.

During the second half of the nineteenth century coal production in South Wales expanded considerably. Between 1870 and 1890 the annual output of the South Wales coalfield rose from 13.5 million tons to 29.4 million tons because of the growth in demand for the steam-coal of the Rhondda Valley. Exports especially increased, and the development of the railways between the pits and the coastal towns helped to advance them even more. This trade was not shared equally amongst the Welsh ports. During the early 1840's cargoes of steam-coal had largely departed from the harbours of Llanelly and Swansea, but after 1850 other ports became more important. It was found that the steam-coal mined in the hinterland of Cardiff and Newport had greater quality and could be obtained more abundantly than the output of seams further west. These ports forged ahead of Swansea, particularly as large quantities of anthracite coal were not exported from the West Glamorgan coalfield until the 1880's. In 1887 annual exports of coal from Cardiff exceeded 7.5 million tons, in comparison with 2.2 million tons from Newport and 1.3 million tons from Swansea. Cardiff became more important than Newport because of the better dock accommodation provided by the Marquis of Bute for ocean and coastal vessels. The early introduction of railways to link the Bute West Dock to the mines maintained this position which was gained in 1848 and was never lost.

Although steam-coal was the chief commodity shipped from the South Wales ports after 1860, other materials were also handled in varying quantities. Iron, steel, tinplates, copper and patent fuel were exported; iron-ore, timber and general merchandise were imported. Most of these trades were still important in 1900, but the shipment of iron decreased before 1870 because of the exhaustion of local iron-ore supplies, competition from firms in the north-east of England and the gradual replacement of iron by steel. New processes for the manufacture of steel were eventually adopted by many Welsh works, and by the 1880's steel was the second most important commodity shipped from Newport and Cardiff. In addition, the development of the steel industry led to an increased import trade at these ports. As the Bessemer Converter and the Siemens-Martin open-hearth furnace proved unable to satisfactorily remove the phosphorous contained within local ores, companies were forced to purchase non-phosphoric ore from Spain. Although Sidney Gilchrist-Thomas later discovered the means to eliminate this element in the converter, the iron-ore trade was not impaired and iron-ore remained the major import of the Welsh ports. In 1897 734,131 tons were imported at Cardiff, 657,712 tons at Newport, and large quantities also arrived at Swansea.

The export of tinplates was chiefly confined to the port of Swansea during the second half of the nineteenth century because of the concentration of most tinplate works in West Wales. It was an important trade: in 1890 421,797 tons of tinplates and sheets were exported, largely to the United States of America. However, the McKinley Tariff introduced by the American Republican Party in 1891 gradually curtailed the export of tinplates to the U.S.A., and led to the depression of the industry in South Wales. At Swansea, too, the shipment of copper declined after 1890 as a result of the development of copper smelting works in South America, the U.S.A. and Australia. Instead of exporting copper ore to West Wales for smelting, foreign mineowners decided increasingly to smelt it locally, because of the mono-polistic practices of Swansea industrialists. The port of Swansea fortunately, though, did not rely completely upon the copper and tinplate trades; it retained its considerable coal trade, and continued to import other commodities.

As a result of the growth of trade, mechanical appliances were introduced on the waterfronts of South Wales during the nineteenth century. At the main ports hydraulic equipment was used to hoist coal wagons and to tip their contents over shutes into vessels, and cranes on the quaysides and

6

power-driven winches on board ships conveyed goods between the hold and deck. Yet, despite these developments, mechanical equipment was used to move only bulk cargoes, for a large and inexpensive labour force was employed to carry freight across the deck and along the quays to the warehouses or railway wagons.

On the waterfronts of South Wales, workmen were hired by a large number of employers. At the chief ports the men who tipped coal from the quay-sides into ships were employed by the dock companies and the Swansea Harbour Trust; those who trimmed the coal (that is, those who distributed coal evenly in the holds and bunkers) on board ships were hired directly by the coal companies or through an agent appointed by them. Port workers who handled iron ore and general cargoes were hired by the dock companies, traders and industrial firms which owned works near to the waterside. Some of these men were also engaged by local contractors and sub-contractors, but this varied after 1890. Whereas the Barry Railway Company and the Swansea Harbour Trust increased the number of port workers they directly employed, the dock companies at Newport and Cardiff continued to contract out a part of their trade.

Port labour was mainly engaged on a casual basis during the nineteenth century, because of fluctuations of trade, weather and tide variations, and the consequential irregularity in the amount of work available. Although the introduction of the steamship led to a more uniform distribution of the volume of work throughout the year, a lack of employment opportunities was experienced intermittently on the waterfront[3]. The hiring of men by a large number of concerns helped to increase under-employment even more, for each employer required the daily attendance of many labourers in order to avoid delays during peak periods of business. The selection of men at numerous independent hiring centres instead of at one central stand encouraged more labourers than were necessary to come to the port and increased the number unemployed. Firms did engage some permanent men for weekly periods, but they largely relied upon the calling-on system for their main supply of labour. In the ports of South Wales this involved the firms' foremen choosing employees from large groups of labourers who had assembled on the quays. It was a degrading method. According to Ben Tillett, the General Secretary of the Dockers' Union,

> A foreman or contractor walks up and down with the air of a dealer in a cattle-market, picking and choosing from a crowd of men, who in their eagerness to obtain employment, trample each other underfoot, and where like beasts they fight for the chances of a day's work.[4]

Even though the handling of goods at the ports of the Principality was carried out chiefly on a casual basis, a regular labour force was engaged. These men constantly sought employment at the docks and wharves, refused to accept subsidiary occupations, and applied most frequently for work at a particular hiring centre. Although they were sometimes taken on by other firms, they were generally unwilling to work in different sections of the port. Their regular attendance at calling-on stands was encouraged by the employers who required a ready supply of men familiar with the particular tasks available, and the dockers themselves felt that it was necessary to become familiar with a company's foreman in order to obtain employment. Foremen at Newport and Cardiff, for instance, often gave preference to friends and to workers who supplied them with cigarettes and beer.

In spite of their constant attendance at the hiring-centres, the number of regulars at each port is very difficult to calculate. Trade fluctuated periodically, and dock workers were often under-employed. During seasons of depression in other industries they were forced to compete with building and agricultural labourers who sought supplementary employment. Moreover, many regular port workers had been employed in other trades and professions before drifting to the quays. Although the Census of Population of 1891 recorded that 682 dock and quay labourers were residing in Newport, 989 at Cardiff and 614 at Swansea, the validity of these figures is questionable, because workers who were unemployed at the time of the returns were probably not included in this survey. These totals also fail to reveal the proportion of individuals engaged in the different sections of port work. Port labourers, as we shall see, not only worked at a particular centre, but also confined themselves to certain tasks.

Despite their low occupational status, waterside employees had various skills and specialised in their work. Important distinctions in fact existed in port work, the most significant of which was between the workers on the ship and those on the shore. Ship workers handled all goods on board the vessel, and arranged and operated the winches and other equipment; shore labourers concentrated upon moving cargo from the quays to the warehouses. This was the custom on every waterfront as ship and shore workers were separate groups which experienced little interchange. Their division was not artificial but evolved because ship work was recognised as the highest grade of activity at the waterfront. This distinction largely derived from the important procedures undertaken during the stowing of ocean-going vessels, for workers on board ship had to ensure that goods would not move dangerously at sea and would be accessible on delivery. Ship workers in South Wales discharged merchandise, too, but this required less responsibility and was less remunerative than stowing.

The conveyance of goods by shore workers from the quays to the warehouses and railway wagons involved less skill, risk and rapidity than was needed to handle cargo on board ship and was not so highly paid. Yet the efforts of shore workers were not completely devoid of proficiency and perseverance. The receiving of merchandise at the ship's rail and the sorting, piling and removal of items by hand trucks to the storage buildings or sidings were accomplished by different labourers at various rates of pay. Whereas the

8

trucking of goods was undertaken by the lowest casual, the placing of materials into piles and railway wagons needed greater experience and ability. Regular employees performed these specialised jobs and were reluctant to accept subordinate activities.

In addition to carrying out particular tasks, many dock, wharf and warehouse workers concentrated upon handling certain goods. In South Wales coal trimmers, deal runners, timber porters, grain workers and iron-ore workers were some of the main groups that specialised **(see Glossary)**. They formed regular gangs and tried to exclude outsiders, who they called "scrap-heap men", from employment. Labourers who moved bulk cargoes such as coal, timber and grain acted in this way because their work demanded considerable strength and technique, and the wage-rates were higher than for other cargoes. Even the general goods porters, who normally comprised the least skilled workers, tried to concentrate upon carrying the merchandise of a particular firm in order to obtain regular work and to achieve some social status. But such specialisation was detrimental to the labourer: it reduced his mobility, increased under-employment and contributed to the poverty and hardship which characterised port work throughout the nineteenth century.

Although proficient men such as coal trimmers had some bargaining power, they were largely unorganised because of their frequent under-employment. Whereas skilled workmen in carpentry and engineering set up craft organisations before 1860, mass unionism was not successfully established at the ports of South Wales until the late 1880's. The impetus for this development was generated by the growth of trade and the London dock strike of 1889. At London,

> The conditions of '89 were such that open revolt was entered upon by men, who for years fawned and trembled in the presence of warehouse keepers and foremen, toadies of a rotten system, which exploited the labour and wages of the men unchecked.[5]

It is the spread of this revolt to South Wales that we must now examine.

NOTES

1. Monmouthshire Canal Company folder, Monmouthshire Collection, Newport (Gwent) Reference Library.

2. Ibid.

3. At Newport, for example, the highest number of men employed on any one day during 1937 was 548 (on 29th June); the lowest number was 3 (on 12th May). On the busiest day 196 men were idle.

4. A Docker (Ben Tillett), *The Dock Labourers' Bitter Cry* (London, 1889), p.2.

5. *Dockers' Record,* June-July, 1921, p.6.

1. They came to the opening of the New Tredegar Arms, Newport

2. This is a view of the Old Town Dock, Newport, opened in 1842. It is from a drawing by J.F. Mullock (1818-92), and seems to have been made about the middle of the century

3. The Bute East Dock, Cardiff, during the 1890's: a view taken from the dock entrance looking north, and showing a ship being loaded at the coal tips

4. A pit-head scene in a South Wales valley

5. The coal tips at the Queen Alexandra Docks, Cardiff, in 1907. Cory Brothers were coalowners, and major exporters at the port

6. Loading patent fuel on the South Wales waterfront

7. Unloading pitwood at Barry Docks in c. 1911. Dockers on shore who carried the wood across the railway track and piled it in stacks were paid approximately eight shillings a day

BUTE DOCKS COMPANY.

NOTICE.

Certain Coal Tippers and others in the employ of the Bute Docks Company having ceased work without assigning any reason or giving any notice, the Company hereby give notice to their Workmen that they require all persons in their employ to give due notice before terminating their engagement, and that any Workman leaving without the notice which he ought to give may be proceeded against for damages; and further, as indicated by notice dated 1st August, 1890, **all Labour at the Bute Docks must be regarded as absolutely free** and that no preference will be given either to Unionists or Non Unionists, and particularly that the Company cannot directly or indirectly recognise any attempt to put pressure upon other employers or workmen as to the terms upon which they are to carry on their business.

W THOMAS LEWIS,
General Manager.

5th February, 1891.

8. A warning to strikers. The Bute Docks Company posted this notice concerning the conditions of employment during the Cardiff coal tippers dispute of 1891

Chapter 1
The Waterloo of Labour

The formation of the Dock, Wharf, Riverside and General Labourers' Union and its development in South Wales, 1889-90.

In August 1889 labourers at docks and wharves throughout the port of London struck for higher wages and better conditions. Except for those workers who were members of a small organisation formed in 1887, the Tea Operatives' and General Labourers' Association, they were largely disorganised and lacked finances. The dockers, however, were helped considerably by Ben Tillett, the Secretary of the Tea Operatives' Association, and his members who undertook the tasks of submitting claims, conducting picket operations and distributing relief. They also benefited from the support of other societies, the valuable assistance of Tom Mann and John Burns, exceptional public sympathy, and donations from Australia. This support proved decisive. The employers capitulated after five weeks, and the strikers achieved the "Dockers' Tanner" (6d. an hour was the new day rate) and a guaranteed minimum of four hours' work for every hired labourer.

As a result of the London dock strike the Tea Operatives' Association grew considerably, and by September 1889 had recruited 20,000 members from all sections of the waterfront. Nonetheless, Tillett felt that it was an inadequate structure for retaining support at London and enlisting members in the provinces. During the dispute it had been forced to function with an insufficient branch and district framework, and its title did not represent many of the new members. At a meeting held in September 1889 the organisation was thus renamed the Dock, Wharf, Riverside and General Labourers' Union of Great Britain and Ireland, (D.W.R.G.L.U.), and officials were elected.

Its members chose leaders who had played an important part in the dock dispute and who had much experience of waterfront conditions. The General Secretary, Ben Tillett, had previously been a sailor and riverside labourer; the two organisers were Tom McCarthy who had been Secretary of the Stevedores' Union in London until the end of the dock strike and Harry Orbell, a former furniture-maker and dock worker. Only the elected President of the union, Tom Mann, was unfamiliar with the waterside industry, for he was an engineer by trade.

Despite his inexperience of port traditions, Mann played an important part in the drafting of the constitution by persuading the union's officials to establish a centralised structure. Rejecting the expense and vulnerability of branch autonomy, the representatives of the Dock, Wharf, Riverside Union (or Dockers' Union as it was more popularly known) decided that the collection of funds, the declaration of strikes and the formation of branches should be the responsibility of the Executive Council at their central office in Mile End Road, London. The Executive Council was also instructed to supervise the management of branches which could hold meetings in school rooms or coffee houses but not public houses as " much beer and much business never go together".[1] Branch officials were encouraged to form district committees and were eligible for selection to the Delegate Council which would meet annually to appoint the Executive Council, revise the constitution and act as a court of appeal.

The consolidation of waterside unionism in London coincided with a dramatic growth in industrial unrest and the formation of societies which recruited workers from many industries. In Britain during 1889 over 1,200 stoppages occurred, and approximately 3.7 million working days were lost because of strikes. According to H. Llewellyn Smith and Vaughan Nash,

> A great awakening has come all over the country, labour is reorganising itself and the spirit of unionism is extending to many trades - skilled and unskilled - to which it had never been at all or successfully applied.[2]

In South Wales, for instance, sadlers, blacksmiths, shop assistant., hairdressers and other workmen formed societies in the following months; and even the neglected wives of Cardiff suggested the formation of a union, the Amalgamated Society of Distressed Wives, for protection against the violent behaviour of their drunken husbands. Working-class associations, though, were not formed solely as a result of the London dock strike, for some organisations were established before August 1889. They were influenced by the same trade boom which later encouraged the dock workers themselves to combine. Nevertheless, the dock strike did help to intensify labour agitation, because it emphasised the benefits obtainable from membership of a trade union. As the *Labour Elector* explained,

> If these men can combine and succeed, no class of workmen however poor their pay or casual their employment need despair of obtaining an immediate alleviation of their lot.[3]

Port labourers in provincial ports were especially influenced by the success of the London men, and attempted to improve their own wages and conditions. Their militancy encouraged Tillett to enrol them and to transform his London-based society into a national organisation.

The development of the Dockers' Union during the autumn months of 1889 was largely unresisted by firms on the waterfront. Unwilling to disrupt trade and incur losses similar to those of the London dock companies, employers quickly capitulated and granted wage increases to union members. Branches were set up at Hull, Southampton, East Anglia, the Medway towns, Bristol, Gloucester, Bridgewater and the ports of South Wales. Their main opposition came initially from locally established unions such as the Cardiff Coal Trimmers' Association at Cardiff and the National Amalgamated Labourers' Union of Great Britain and Ireland which had members at Newport, Cardiff and Swansea. These unions had been established before the London dock strike of 1889, and did not welcome competition from the Dockers' Union.

The Cardiff Coal Trimmers' Association was formed at the Great Western Coffee Tavern, Cardiff, in April 1888, because of the employers' persistent infringement of a tariff which had been negotiated in 1879. The Association later enrolled members at Barry and Penarth and had 1100 members in 1889, but it rejected large-scale expansion and attempted to recruit only regular coal trimmers and coal foremen at these ports and enforce the closed shop. Like many unions the Association had a central fund and paid officials, but it adopted an unusual method of subscription: weekly contributions were levied by poundage from members' wages by their foremen, many of whom were union officials. Furthermore, although the Association paid accident benefit and death allowance, dispute pay was not given. Thus, although the men's employment situation on the quays was safeguarded, their ability to strike was limited.

The formation of the National Amalgamated Labourers' Union was closely linked with the development of the Seamen's Union in South Wales. During the autumn months of 1888 branches of Havelock Wilson's National Amalgamated Sailors' and Firemen's Union were opened in Cardiff by John Gardner and at Newport by Albert Kenny. Kenny also assisted the society at Dublin, Cork and Whitehaven, but he left to establish a labourers' association at Cardiff in June 1889. His National Amalgamated Labourers' Union was soon extended throughout the city and enrolled engineering workers, dry dock labourers, builders' labourers, patent fuel workers and waterside employees. Subsequently a union of trimmers, tippers, cranemen and dry dock workers which was formed at Swansea in December 1889 by Harry Williams also affiliated, and branches of the N.A.L.U. were established at Newport, Cadoxton and Chepstow. Aided by the growth of trade the union's strength rose to 5,531 in December 1890, and it negotiated pay increases for its members without becoming involved in disputes. Although the organisation had a strike fund, its leaders condemned stoppages. T. J. O'Keefe, the secretary of the Cardiff district, wrote,

> Proud may we feel when we understand that it was not through ruinous contention or strife that we gained such advances, but by those peaceable methods before mentioned and a surety of the employers' recognition of our union.[4]

Albert Kenny also stressed the importance of benefit payments which, he felt, were essential if his union was to become "a solid permanent institution". As a result the N.A.L.U. offered its members sickness, strike, funeral and accident benefits, legal assistance, and travelling grants to further their search for employment. An Executive Committee controlled the funds and forwarded the men's demands, and the Annual General Meeting of branch representatives elected officials and altered the rules.

Despite the strength of the Coal Trimmers' Association and the N.A.L.U. at Cardiff, the Dockers' Union formed a branch in the city in November 1889. Riggers, hobblers, patent fuel men, iron-ore labourers, trimmers and workers at the Spillers' Flour Mill joined, but its membership did not increase significantly until the visit of Ben Tillett on 30th November. A torchlight procession of dockers took place, and Tillett marched at its head through Cardiff's main streets to the city centre, where he invited workers to join his organisation. Several branches were later set up, and a thousand workmen were enrolled during the next few months. Each port labourer paid 2/6d. to join the union and contributed 2d. per week. If involved in a dispute which was approved by the Executive Council, he was eligible to receive 10/- per week strike payment, but the Dockers' Union was unable to give sickness and funeral benefits because of the low contributions.

In spite of its success in Cardiff, the Dockers' Union was not at first welcomed in Swansea. When Tillett and John Burns visited the town in February 1890 local contractors opposed them, and hired thugs to disrupt their activities. Placards were displayed advising Swansea labourers "to turn them London agitators out", and Tillett and Burns received a noisy reception at a mass meeting. Tillett recalled,

> Boozers, bullies and bruisers were sent to assault me violently and they came to the Drill Hall with various emanations and accretions they had taken from the roadside. These were the preparations for my reception. When I got into the Drill Hall, I was howled at from end to end . . . We didn't give a two-penny hang for the whole caboosh and that very night the Dockers' Union was inaugurated.[5]

The union in fact flourished within the Swansea district, and Dockers' officials such as Tom McCarthy and Harry Orbell were subsequently well-received at public meetings.

By May 1890 the Dockers' members in Swansea considered themselves strong enough to take on their employers. Encouraged also by the growth of trade they drew up a petition demanding an increase in wages, the replacement of boy winch drivers by men, and a guarantee of two shillings pay for dockers who were asked to work at night. The union's representatives later negotiated a settlement with the employers, and concessions were obtained for dockers involved in tinplate, copper and ballast discharging. According to Tillett, "the Swansea masters were as fair and as reasonable a class of men as he had ever met."[6] Only the Graigola Patent Fuel Company refused to grant increases, but it soon capitulated when a mass strike at the port was declared by the men on 16th June. However, against Tillett's advice, the labourers who struck refused to return to work and rejected the terms which had been previously negotiated. The General Secretary appealed to these workers to consider the concessions, but "if they were ready for the fight he was ready, and would cheerfully enter into it."[7] The men's determination prevailed, and they remained on strike, eventually forcing the companies to accept their substantial demands three days later. Even though the port workers had acted contrary to union policy, they were congratulated by their officials. Harry Orbell remarked that,

He had been in no town which he could compare so favourably with as Swansea during a strike. There was an entire absence of foul language, and there had been very little drink.[8]

Although the Dockers' Union obtained mass support at ports such as Swansea because of strikes, its officials soon emphasised the need to prevent unnecessary stoppages by the establishment of conciliation and arbitration boards with the employers. Tillett and Mann argued that strikes should be avoided, "Wherever possible and only entered into after other efforts at a settlement have failed."[9] The Dockers' leaders also stressed the rule that members would receive strike pay only if they left work with the permission of the Executive Council. Their policy of moderation was adopted for a purpose: they wished to offer a guarantee of efficient and uninterrupted work to firms in order to persuade them to grant preference of employment to their members. This was essential for the organisation to retain its numerical strength and to achieve greater stability of employment on the waterfront. As companies engaged workers on a casual basis to perform relatively unskilled tasks, the closed shop was the most effective means for the union to improve the wages of its members and to enforce discipline. Restriction of entry into the organisation was advocated by some officials, but this proved inadequate as businesses could still engage outsiders. The most satisfactory method of excluding non-union labour was to gain recognition from the employers, permission to check union cards at the calling-on stands, and the recruitment of foremen who selected the men. Yet large waterside concerns refused to accept the monopoly of union labour, for they believed that the employment of other workmen was needed to ensure the rapid dispatch of shipping and that the closed shop would lead to inefficiency. Their resistance was intensified by the readiness of the Dockers' rank and file to strike whenever non-unionists were hired. Despite Mann and Tillett's advice, members were not always prepared to apply to their leaders for an investigation of their complaints; they often struck and then asked for financial assistance which the Executive Council was forced to provide, because it did not wish to lose their support.

Following the strike at Swansea, the position of the Dockers' Union was strengthened at the docks without the occurrence of disputes. As the employers were benefiting from the growth of trade, they readily agreed to the union's demands to exclude women corn workers and other non-unionists from the waterfront. Its membership also increased, and in November 1890 the Dockers had over 4650 members in the Swansea area. Its growth was undertaken largely at the expense of Albert Kenny's organisation. Before Tillett's visit to the town the N.A.L.U. had over 2000 members at the docks; in December 1890 only 380 remained. Except for the coal trimmers, tippers and hydraulic cranemen who remained loyal to Harry Williams and Kenny, most port labourers changed unions. They were influenced by the substantial gains obtained by the Dockers' Union and its refusal to recognise their tickets.

In the Swansea hinterland, Dockers' leaders also formed branches at factories in order to increase their funds and to obtain regular contributions during waterfront strikes. The Port Tennant Chemical Works, Cape Copper Works, Morfa Copper Works and Llandore Tube Works were organised, and the union obtained wage increases and tried to enforce the closed shop. It was resisted only at the Morfa Copper Works where six members were dismissed in July 1890. The management denied allegations of victimisation, but refused to meet union representatives who were forced to retaliate. A strike was declared at the factory, and Harry Orbell was sent to Swansea by Tillett to organise the men and to persuade the employers to conciliate. A settlement was eventually reached, largely because of the efforts of a local copper worker, James Wignall, who arranged a meeting with the directors. At this discussion arbitration was agreed upon, and the strike ended on 30th September. The arbitrators later offered an acceptable solution which helped to preserve the Dockers' position at Morfa: the men were to ask for reinstatement and were to be employed on the same seniority as in July. Wignall himself also benefited from the strike, for his activities impressed Tillett who wrote,

> My first experience of Wignall was on a slag-heap just outside of Swansea. He had obtained some notoriety not only as a copper worker but as a parson. He was pouring forth unction with all his courage and vehemence. I thought he would make a very good agitator.[10]

Wignall thus achieved prominence in the Dockers' Union, and was appointed district secretary in Swansea in 1892 and national organiser in 1900.

Although Tillett's union grew at Swansea and considerably weakened the N.A.L.U., this did not occur at Newport. A branch was established on the Newport waterside in February 1890 but its progress was disappointing. In November 1890 only 712 workmen were affiliated, because insufficient attention was paid by the Cardiff-based district officials of the Dockers' Union to the port. The N.A.L.U. also took advantage of the Dockers' inadequate organisation and obtained substantial gains for its members. As a result it retained its hold on the riverside workers and general dock labourers at Newport, and only the coal trimmers and tippers at the docks joined the Dockers' Union.

The Newport coal trimmers, like their Swansea counterparts, thus did not join the same organisation as the general dock labourers. The coal trimmers were the most skilful workers on the waterfront, and probably believed that the encroachment of other labourers at their calling-on stands would be better prevented by joining a different union to them. Their affiliation to the Dockers' Union in fact led to conflict with the N.A.L.U. at Newport, because both organisations demanded preference of employment for their members. Frequent stoppages occurred at the port, and forced the unions to agree eventually to allow their members to work together in all South Wales towns and to act jointly in trade disputes. Union strife was halted by this settlement, but it proved impossible for either body to enforce discipline and to keep a stable membership. As workers were not obliged to show their cards to representatives of the other society, outsiders could be excluded only if challenged simultaneously by officials of both unions. Unionists were also able to transfer, and this provided a suitable alternative for those who had fallen behind with their subscriptions.

Despite being a general labourers' organisation, the D.W.R.G.L.U. did not organise many workers from manufacturing industries at Newport and the surrounding area. In the Gwent valleys branches were formed only at the Ebbw Vale Steel and Coal Company and the Blaenavon Works, and at Cardiff only the gasworkers and a small union of hauliers and porters were enrolled. Although willing to recruit these and other industrial groups such as the Swansea copper workers who sought the protection of unionism, the Dockers' Union principally catered for workmen at the docks and river wharves. The union needed to increase its central funds by opening new branches, but it was more essential to protect the casual port labourers who were vulnerable to blacklegging and to concentrate upon obtaining the monopoly of work.

At Cardiff, in particular, the Dockers' Union made a vigorous effort to achieve the closed shop. Though it failed to weaken significantly the N.A.L.U., which retained the support of riggers, tugboatmen, patent fuel workers and dock labourers, the union organised over 800 coal trimmers who were members of the Cardiff Coal Trimmers' Association. The coal trimmers were dissatisfied with their rates of pay and especially with the officials of the Coal Trimmers' Association who were not prepared to negotiate for wage improvements. Most of these officials were foremen, the salaried servants of the coal companies which profited by keeping wages down. As a result the coal trimmers joined Tillett's union which agreed to formulate a new tariff; but they were compelled at the same time to remain members of the Trimmers' Association, for the foremen continued to subtract subscriptions from their wages and helped to preserve the strength of the Association. The Association was also aided by the attitude of the employers who recognised its leaders but refused to deal with the Dockers' Union. Although local concerns were not antagonised by the moderate demands of the small craft union, they opposed the Dockers' request for the closed shop and substantial wage increases.

The largest employing concern at the port of Cardiff was the Bute Docks Company which managed the docks and railway facilities. Its General Manager, Sir William Thomas Lewis, handled all matters of industrial relations, and was also Chairman of the Sliding-Scale Committee which he had helped to form in 1875 to regulate wages and to prevent disputes in the South Wales coal industry. Lewis co-operated with miners' representatives such as William Abraham ("Mabon") and was generally regarded as a philanthropist, but he had strong views concerning the methods of trade union organisation. Though he did not object to the South Wales and Monmouthshire Miners' Federation, he denounced any society which demanded the allegiance of every workman and always upheld "the rights of workmen to be non-unionists or unionists as they thought proper"[11] Lewis was backed after 1889 by many Cardiff merchants who regarded the dock workers' and seamen's demands for the closed shop as totally unacceptable, and their support made him even more reluctant to compromise.

Despite Lewis views, the coal tippers' and coal trimmers' branches of the Dockers' Union in Cardiff in July 1890 submitted a claim for increased wages, a reduction in hours and the exclusion of non-unionists from the quays. The men were supported by Ben Tillett who travelled from London to Wales to assist them. He stressed that,

> Our policy is adverse to strike but if, after timely notice has been given, the folk in authority refuse to make the desired concessions, we shall fight to the bitter end. We are sure to win, for not only have we the power to close the Bute Docks, but . . . we are able to stop the docks at Swansea, Newport, Bristol and even those of Sharpness and Gloucester.[12]

Tillett proposed that the employers should discuss the men's grievances with his union at a conference, and declared that formal notice would be given by his members only if the meeting failed. This suggestion, nonetheless, was rejected by the Bute Docks Company, which was also involved with the claims of its enginemen and signalmen for a guaranteed week's pay and a 60 hour weekly maximum. Along with the Rhymney, Taff Vale and Barry Railway Companies, it had already received notices from the railwaymen's union, the Amalgamated Society of Railway Servants. The seriousness of this situation led the directors of the Bute Docks Company to resist all demands, and discussions were held with representatives of the other companies involved. At these meetings the dock and railway questions were examined, and Lewis' decision to uphold the status quo on the waterfront was unanimously approved.

Sir William Lewis' policy was also endorsed by employing concerns at the port of Cardiff. The Cardiff Shipowners' Association and the Cardiff Chamber of Commerce passed resolutions which approved the firm stand of the Bute Docks Company, and William Riley, the President of the Chamber of Commerce, emphasised that the merchants would endure a general lock-out rather than concede the men's claims. Consequently Lewis continued to refuse to meet Dockers' officials, and was prepared to discuss issues only with the port workers themselves. Yet, despite the Bute Dock Company's attitude, Tillett did not recommend industrial action, and instead suggested arbitration. But his efforts to obtain a settlement were curtailed by the declaration of a strike by the Amalgamated Society of Railway Servants on 6th August. Unwilling to involve his union in a costly dispute and risk defeat, he announced the postponement of his members' claims until the end of the stoppage.

Even though the railway companies capitulated a week later, the Dockers' Union was still unable to achieve advances for most of its members in Cardiff. The union obtained concessions from smaller concerns, but the Bute Docks Company remained uncompromising. The railway settlement had enlarged the company's wage bill, and Lewis was reluctant to allow further increases. He also continued to refuse to recognise union officials and to oppose the introduction of the closed shop at the docks. Lewis believed that he could solve the problems of the waterfront by establishing a wages board similar to the Sliding-Scale Committee in the coal trade. In September 1890 he devised a scheme, the Bristol Channel Docks Association of Employers and Workmen, but his proposal was rejected by the unions. The General Manager's suggestion that non-unionists should become members of the Board was unacceptable to union officials who argued that the Cardiff Trades Council should elect the workmen's representatives. The issue of union monopoly at the Bute Docks thus became a stalemate: the Dockers' Union had a large membership, but its leaders appreciated the strength of the dock company and were reluctant to force a conflict. This situation was not resolved until February 1891, when they and the employers clashed over the "free" labour issue.

At Newport, on the other hand, Tillett's organisation did not face such strong opposition from the employers. The Alexandra (Newport and South Wales) Docks and Railway Company was less hostile to the issue of preference of employment, because it was reluctant to lose trade as a result of strikes. When the whole labour force struck in July 1890 because of the arrival of a vessel with a non-union crew, the company immediately agreed to the men's request that the ship be removed from the hoists to the buoys, and the vessel remained in the middle of the dock until the captain recruited trade unionists. In July 1890 the Newport trimmers also negotiated a piece-work price list for trimming coal and coke, and three months later Henry Seer, their district secretary, obtained representation upon a Board of Conciliation. These were important advantages which the Dockers' branches at Cardiff did not achieve because of the hostility of the Bute Docks Company.

The employers' counter-attack 1891-92.

During 1889 and 1890 the development of the Dockers' Union in South Wales had been affected to a large extent by the growth of trade. Many workers had been recruited (by January 1891 5,862 men had joined at Swansea, 3,020 at Cardiff and 804 at Newport), and they had obtained regular employment and achieved wage advances. However, this position was not maintained because trade declined, the number of outsiders at the hiring centres increased, and interest in union affairs waned. The national strength of the Dockers' Union fell from 57,000 in 1890 to 22,913 in 1892. Yet its influence did not decline uniformly in each port: whereas mass unionism on the Cardiff waterfront was moribund by June 1893, the two Newport branches shared over a thousand members. Although the decline in trade partly accounts for a reduction in membership, it does not explain such diversities.

The survival of the union after 1891, in fact, was largely dependent upon the attitude of the employer. Influenced by the decline of trade and over-supply of labour **(see Appendix One)**, some waterside concerns tried to recover the financial concessions which they had granted in 1889 and to destroy the union's monopoly of work. Preference of employment for its members had led to inefficiency, because, lacking strong competition from outsiders at the calling-on stands, workers had become slack and over-confident. Timber firms in the Bristol Channel area, for instance, complained,

> In former days we used to call them deal runners, but there is no run in them now - all they care to do is to skunk, and as to running, they don't even go a decent walking pace.[13]

In their stand against the union, employers were assisted after September 1890 by the Shipping Federation which made available to them an alternative labour force. The Shipping Federation was formed to smash the National Amalgamated Sailors' and Firemen's Union, but it subsequently also opposed dock labourers' unions which became involved in the seamen's struggle for the closed shop.

The formation of the National Amalgamated Sailors' and Firemen's Union in July 1887 by J. Havelock Wilson did not initially concern many shipowners, for they realised that the recruitment of seamen was difficult and believed that Wilson's organisation would quickly collapse. Nevertheless, the shipowners' attitude changed when the growth of trade led to the expansion of the union and increased its bargaining power. The Sailors' Union picketed the shipping offices where workers were hired and tried to prevent the entry of non-unionists. Moreover, it reached an understanding with the National Certificated Officers' Union of Great Britain and Ireland, a society of ship's officers which was established during this period, that the officers who helped to select sailors at the hiring centres would employ only members of the Seamen's Union. Wilson also became General Manager of the Officers' Union, and he instructed seamen not to sail in ships whose officers refused to belong to this organisation. His decision alarmed shipowners so considerably that they held a national conference at London in August 1890 and decided to firmly resist the seamen's policies. As a result of this meeting they formed the Shipping Federation a month later.

The Shipping Federation, which was managed by George A. Laws, was based in London. All shipowners were eligible to join, and district committees were set up at various ports including Newport and Cardiff. It achieved much support from large concerns, and represented over 7 million tons of sea-going vessels in 1891. Wilson claimed that it was merely "a federation on paper",[14] but the Shipping Federation soon became aggressive and announced that the principle of "liberty of contract" would be upheld, masters and non-unionists would be protected, and crews would be obtained for shipping companies at market rates during strikes. Seamen were also issued with tickets which gave their holders preference of employment provided they agreed to work alongside union and non-union men alike. The Federation enforced this ticket in February 1891 by declaring that only men with tickets were to be employed, and they were to be engaged on board ship. Its policies were a direct threat to the National Amalgamated Sailors' and Firemen's Union which vigorously intensified its campaign to achieve the closed shop. But the seamen were fighting a losing battle, because they lacked the vast resources of the Federation which sent depot ships housing blackleg labour (that is, men brought in to take the place of strikers) to break strikes on the waterfront.

The Shipping Federation was strongly resisted at the Bristol Channel ports where the Seamen's Union had many members. Vessels carrying non-union crews were boycotted and the shipping offices were picketed. In dockland public houses and outside the Shipping Federation offices in Newport and Cardiff blacklegs were beaten until "their faces and other parts of them (were) black and blue and like jellies".[15] The seamen were assisted by local officials of the Dockers, the National Amalgamated Labourers' Union, and a small society of riggers, hobblers and boatmen. Along with the Seamen's Union they formed in January 1891 a labour federation, the Federated Trades and Labour Unions, and agreed to oppose the employment of non-union labour at sea and to participate in disputes in every Welsh port. Dockers' representatives became involved in the seamen's struggle because they opposed the coercion of fellow unionists by the shipowners and because they feared that the Shipping Federation's labour force would eventually be used to weaken the position of their own members. The Shipping Federation, Tillett felt, was

An aggressive body who, while whining about the brutality of trade unionists have yet armed men with bludgeons, revolvers and a supply of intoxicants to be guilty of the worst ruffianism - gangs of half-drunken men who have resisted with violence men fighting for ... the principle of fair remuneration.[16]

While the Dockers' branches assisted the Seamen's Union, they also continued to press for wage improvements. In December 1890 the Cardiff coal tippers formulated fresh demands which they submitted to the Bute Docks Company. Yet, even though the union dropped its request for the monopoly of work on the waterfront, the Bute Docks Company still refused to negotiate with its officials and to grant increases. The return on dock investment in the 1880's was unsatisfactory, and the Company could not afford to increase labour costs. Moreover, its directors were very concerned about the decline of coal shipments at Cardiff following the opening of Barry Dock in 1889, and were convinced that they should take a firm stand against the "new unions" because of the seamen's demands for the closed shop. Their decision was endorsed by other employers at the port who had approved Sir William Lewis' rejection of the dock workers' wage-claim in August 1890.

Despite the employers' attitude, Dockers' officials continued to support Wilson's union and backed its decision to 'black' ships carrying non-union sailors at Cardiff. Harry Orbell, its national organiser, argued that, "The sooner (the workmen) have a go the better, because we shall know where we are"[17], and advised his members to challenge the next ship which entered the port with a non-union crew. But Orbell did not suggest a general strike, since his organisation lacked funds and he merely wished to persuade the employers to negotiate. However, because of the militancy of the rank and file, a major confrontation with the Bute Docks Company was brought about.

The arrival of the *Glen Gelder* at the coal tips of the East Dock, Cardiff on 3rd February, 1891 led to the struggle between the Dockers' Union and the Bute Docks Company. As the ship was manned by non-unionists, six coal tippers were ordered to stop work by Orbell and John Gardner, the Sailors' district secretary, who stressed that the men would load the vessel only if the sailors were replaced by union members. Yet the dock company remained unyielding: at a meeting the following day, Lord Edmund, Hon. H.D. Ryder, W. Sneyd and fellow-directors instructed Sir William Lewis to inform the men that no distinction could be allowed between trade unionist and non-unionist workers, and to replace the six tippers by other labourers and take out summonses against them. The firm's decision was denounced by the tippers and cranemen of the port who struck without consulting Orbell. At a meeting several hours later Orbell was persuaded to give financial support, but he refused to call out the iron-ore men, patent fuel workers and corn porters. The Seamen's Union, nonetheless, adopted a more militant attitude, and, when Havelock Wilson arrived at Cardiff a week later, he told his members not to work.

Although the Dockers' Union had become implicated in a dispute which had originated because of the policies of the Sailors' Union, its leaders realised that other important issues were also involved. Ben Tillett proclaimed that,

24

It was not only the seamen they were fighting for; they were fighting for "free" labour and for the right of recognition.[18]

Cardiff, he stressed was

the only port of any importance in the United Kingdom, where employers had refused to meet men as represented by their trade unions[19].

The Dockers' representatives, though, soon discovered that their aims would not be easily achieved. In the first place, the Bute Docks Company quickly obtained blacklegs to operate the coal tips, and housed and fed them in premises at the waterside. Police guarded the dock gates, and detectives followed bands of strikers throughout the dockland area of "Tiger Bay". In addition, the Shipping Federation provided labourers to man the ships, and it brought a depot ship, the *Speedwell,* to the port. In the second place, the unions lacked the vital support of strategic groups such as the Cardiff Coal Trimmers' Association which decided to trim the coal tipped by the strike-breakers. The unbelligerance of the Association enabled the employers to remain uncompromising. Tom Mann, for instance, tried to settle the dispute on 14th February, but was informed by Lewis that as new hands had been permanently engaged there was nothing to negotiate about.

As a result of Lewis' attitude Mann and Tillett decided to widen the conflict, and they appealed to the Railwaymen, Miners and other unions to support them. Yet, in spite of their request, most organisations refused to prevent the shipment of coal from Cardiff docks. The leaders of the Amalgamated Society of Railway Servants, in particular, wished to preserve industrial peace. The settlement of August 1890 had guaranteed their members a week's wage irrespective of fluctuations in the mineral traffic, provided that such fluctuations were not due to strikes. To avoid participation in the Dockers' stoppage, the Railwaymen's officials followed lengthy constitutional procedures and did not announce their members' refusal to stop work until 14th March. The South Wales and Monmouthshire Miners' Federation, which was also asked to help, similarly employed delaying tactics. It suggested the convening of a general conference of representatives from each trade union in South Wales and Monmouthshire to discuss the dispute and to formulate a settlement. Its advice, however, was accepted by Dockers' delegates who wished to impress the employers with the unity and strength of labour organisations. Tom Mann, especially, realised the possibility of establishing a South Wales Labour Federation, which

would be so powerful that for a certainty, they would be able to secure success by negotiation without resorting to the arbitrament of a strike.[20]

Only Havelock Wilson, the Seamen's leader, criticised the Miners' proposal: he believed that the involvement of other unions in the dispute was unrealistic.

The conference of trade union delegates was held at Cardiff on 3rd and 4th March, and representatives from twenty-nine trade societies and three trade councils attended. They discussed the dispute and selected a deputation which waited upon Sir William Lewis to request the reinstatement of the tippers. According to Havelock Wilson, Lewis received these officials who

> began to tell Sir William all about the strike and what a good thing it would be to have it closed (on their terms of course). Then Sir William in the coolest manner possible said, "To what strike are you referring, gentlemen? It is quite news to me to hear of any strike; the work at the docks is being carried on under absolute normal conditions and we are quite satisfied with the men we have in our employ. Our books will show the men are earning **extraordinary big wages. Of course**", he said, "**I am aware of the fact that some of our poor misguided men have foolishly left their jobs, but**", added Sir William, "**that is their business and not mine**". This terminated the interview, except as a parting shot Sir William said that if the men at any time cared to make application for employment every case would be judged on its merits.[21]

The officials reported the interview to the conference which denounced this rebuff, but the majority of delegates were reluctant to sanction industrial action and decided to send another deputation to the General Manager before a strike was ordered. It was also agreed to recall the conference a week later to review the situation.

The delegates' decision displeased Ben Tillett who wanted immediate support. He attended a mass meeting of colliers at Aberdare on 7th March and asked them to assist his union by halting the coal trade. It was a vain attempt, because the miners were unfamiliar with the problems of organising seafaring labour and lacked sympathy with the sailors' demands for the monopoly of work. Tillett's proposal was overwhelmingly rejected, though the colliers deferred the decision of giving financial assistance to the strikers. Lacking funds and the active support of strategic groups, the Dockers' General Secretary was forced to turn back to the conference of union delegates; yet his efforts to achieve a satisfactory settlement were considerably undermined by a second conference on 12th March. The conference was informed that the Shipping Federation had withdrawn their preference ticket, and delegates unanimously advised a return to work. The South Wales and Monmouthshire Miners' Association also finally decided not to give financial help to the strikers. Consequently, even though Lewis still refused to reinstate the tippers, Dockers' officials were forced to end the dispute two days later. The collapse of the strike led to a reduction of wages for coal tippers, the 'sack' for some dockers, and a general decrease in union membership on the Cardiff waterfront.

Tillett's organisation, on the other hand, did not face such bitter opposition from firms at Newport. The largest concern, the Alexandra (Newport and South Wales) Docks and Railway Company, declined to spend its capital upon defeating the Dockers' Union and the N.A.L.U., because it did not wish to risk losing trade to nearby ports as a result of strikes. Moreover, a prominent director of the company, Sir George Elliott, was the Conservative M.P. for Monmouth Boroughs, and it appears that he did not wish to jeopardise his position by alienating the working classes. The dock company's attitude was very apparent when an incident occurred at Newport similar to that of the *Glen Gelder* dispute. A vessel, the *Rougement,* whose captain intended to hire non-unionists arrived at the Alexandra Dock on 10th February, 1891, and the trimmers and hoistmen who were members of the Dockers' Union refused to load it. In spite of the availability of blackleg labour and the policy of the Bute Docks Company over the closed shop issue, Newport employers did not intervene, and the captain was forced to take the vessel to the East Dock, Cardiff, where it was stowed by Lewis' strike-breakers. The strong influence of trade unionism at the port of Newport thus remained.

Despite the refusal of the Miners' and Railwaymen's organisations to help during the Cardiff strike, the Dockers' and Seamen's Unions subsequently attempted to establish a federation of labour societies in South Wales. A small federation had been formed before the Cardiff strike by the port workers, sailors and riggers, but it was decided to transform this into a larger organisation, the South Wales and Monmouthshire Federation of Trades and Labour Unions. As these unions had been unable by themselves to prevent the hiring of outsiders on the waterfront, their officials hoped that the assistance of other societies would strengthen their position. Provisional rules were soon formulated, and were submitted to a conference of representatives from twenty-one unions in April 1891. They were based upon the constitution of the Federation of Trades and Labour Unions connected with the Shipping and other Industries which had been formed in London four months earlier to defend dockers and seamen against the counter-attack of their employers. These proposals, though, were not accepted by the Miners' and Railwaymen's leaders who were unwilling to be bound by a constitution which would allow the Executive Council of the South Wales Federation to sanction a strike in support of any member. Edward Harford's Amalgamated Society of Railway Servants declined to affiliate; the South Wales and Monmouthshire Miners' Federation joined, but obtained important changes in the draft rules. The representative system was altered in October 1891, and the Miners were given an increased proportion of seats. The strike clause was also modified: henceforth, workers of any trade could not be called out until a ballot of the members of the South Wales and Monmouthshire Federation had been taken and a special general meeting convened. These changes satisfied the Miners who wanted to preserve their Sliding-Scale agreement, but Tillett's organisation had less representation under the new constitution and remained unable to involve other unions in the conflicts of the waterfront.

The counter-attack by employers against the Dockers' Union was not a uniform process. Whereas the action of the Bute Docks Company in February 1891 had caused its membership to decline substantially at Cardiff, some dock labourers and copper workers in Swansea achieved wage increases during 1891. The port of Swansea, nevertheless, did not avoid industrial conflict. A dispute between the copper ore labourers and their employers began on 22nd March, 1892 and lasted for six weeks, because of an attempt by a local firm, Messrs. Bath, to alter the system of discharging ore. The company insisted that steam cranes instead of winches would be used to unload cargoes of Spanish ore, but the men complained that this system would reduce the number of workmen employed and create harmful clouds of dust in the ship's hold. They stopped work, and Messrs. Bath engaged blacklegs to deal with shipments at their wharf.

Bath's strike-breakers worked without incident for several weeks, as the Dockers' Union was anxious to avoid another expensive strike and refused to intervene. The establishment of a "free" labour office by the Swansea Employers' Association in April, however, intensified the dispute, for local employers attempted to register the names of all labourers in search of work and to issue tickets which would give preference of employment to holders. Like the Shipping Federation they believed that union and non-union men should be treated the same and should work together under the terms of their contract.

As they wanted their organisation to have control over hiring procedures, the Dockers' rank and file objected to the employers' attitude and decided to make a determined effort to prevent the "free" labour movement gaining a foothold in Swansea. On 26th April they took a firm stand against the dismissal by H. H. Vivian, a patent fuel company, of five bargemen who had refused to transport cargo which had been handled by the "free" labourers at Messrs. Bath's wharf. Unionists urged Messrs. Vivian to reinstate their employees and in retaliation refused to discharge their goods on the waterfront, but the patent fuel company was uncompromising and hired blackleg labour to unload its materials. The firm's decision considerably angered Dockers' members at the Atlantic fuel works, the Graigola fuel works and the tin sheds who struck in sympathy the same day without the permission of their officials.

Messrs. Vivian's decision to uphold the principle of "free" labour was approved by a number of firms in the area. The Swansea Employers' Association raised a sum of £2000 to obtain "free" labourers from the Shipping Federation, and these men arrived at the port in a depot ship two days later. They received a hostile reception from dockers who attacked Bath's yard and damaged a blackleg's house in Carmarthen Road. Yet these disturbances failed to persuade the employers to capitulate, as they had police support and enough funds to endure a long stoppage. Their strong position was appreciated by Harry Orbell and E. J. Humby, the Dockers' regional organiser, who intervened in the dispute and negotiated a settlement on 4th May. Although wages were not reduced, it was agreed that the employers were to retain the "free" labour office and to hire whoever they wished, and that a local board of conciliation and arbitration was to be established to represent the masters, unionists and non-unionists. These terms largely benefited the employers, but the Dockers' officials disclaimed all responsibility. Humby argued that,

The men had entered that strike purely on their own responsibility. They took the bit between their teeth and had a sort of scratch strike. They explained to the men beforehand the risk they ran, but they in effect told them to mind their own business.[22]

The collapse of the Swansea dock labourers' strike led to a general decline of the Dockers' branches at the port. Their contributions fell from £2,637 in 1891 to £753 in 1893, and the men became very disunited. One local docker wrote,

Unionist members of unskilled labour at the Swansea docks have as much regard for the interests or success of their fellow workmen as Satan has for holy waters.[23]

Furthermore, the agreement between the union and the companies did not represent the culmination of the employers' counter-attack. Only a few months later the Swansea timber firm of T. P. Richards reduced day wages at the port from 7/- to 6/- by obtaining blacklegs from the Shipping Federation and police protection. The action of this firm, though, was not a local phenomenon; it must be seen as part of a concerted effort by members of the Bristol Channel Timber Importers' Association to introduce a uniform minimum wage-rate for discharging timber in the Bristol Channel ports.

The Bristol Channel Timber Importers' Association originated because of the grievances of the Bristol timber merchants. Strikes on the Bristol waterfront in October and November 1889 had forced the merchants to raise their charges for landing and piling wood so considerably that they became the highest in the United Kingdom. The demand for timber also declined after 1889, and imports decreased from 122,036 to 109,025 loads in 1893. The timber importers, as we have seen, largely blamed the inefficiency and belligerence of their workmen for this situation. They also considered the Dockers' demand for the closed shop completely impractical, because foreign shipowners insisted upon discharging cargoes with their own crews. These grievances were not confined to the traders of Bristol; the Bristol Channel Association which was formed in January 1890 embraced the principal ports of South Wales and the West of England. Its members, especially the President, Charles Hoskins Low of Bristol, and the Vice-President, William Riley of Cardiff, were determined to crush militant waterfront unionism and impose a lower rate for unloading timber upon the workers of each port. With the exception of the Shipping Federation, the Association became the strongest and most well-organised body of port employers in the region.

At Bristol the timber merchants took advantage of an irresponsible stoppage by four hundred of their deal runners and enforced a lock-out in November 1892. Sixty "free" labourers from Glasgow and Cardiff were provided by Graeme Hunter who operated a blackleg agency during the 1890's. Throughout the dispute Hunter and his labourers were housed in the employers' premises at the timber yards where they were provided with food, bedding, beer, police protection, and weekly services from the vicar of St. Augustine's, Bristol. Although during the lock-out a number of these labourers were beaten up by militant unionists, the "kill-a-man-a-minute chaps"[24], and great labour demonstrations were held in the city, the timber merchants refused to arbitrate and by June 1893 had imposed their new terms on the Dockers' Union. The union's income subsequently declined, but its six Bristol branches survived because the members of the Bristol Timber Merchants' Association were the only employers who attempted to weaken the organisation at the Bristol and Avonmouth docks after 1891.[25]

At Cardiff, on the other hand, the Dockers' membership declined to an even greater extent, and its income in the district for the second half of 1893 was less than £5. The Bute Docks Company continued to refuse to recognise Dockers' officials, and the timber merchants opened a "free" labour office in the city. Resistance to the union at Cardiff was, in fact, so powerful that, according to Tillett,

> This district is deplorable from a wage-earning stand-point, the most vicious principles stand for gospel among the employers of this district, and the men are pitted against each other in the cruellest fashion, to cut down wages and to otherwise commit industrial suicide. One might say that every interest, commercial, religious, social, political and journalistic are in conspiracy against the men's best interest. The most malignant hatred is directed against the movement generally by all the forces named.[26]

In order to rectify this situation, prominent representatives of the union attempted to reorganise the Cardiff port workers during the summer months of 1893, but they were unsuccessful. Dockers' leaders also tried to persuade members of the South Wales and Monmouthshire Federation of Trades and Labour Unions to resist the establishment of "free" labour exchanges in the city. Several societies gave their support, but the Miners' delegates withdrew from the Federation which was later dissolved. Tillett's organisation thus remained unable to undermine the position of the Cardiff employers, and by 1894 it was moribund in the area.

NOTES

1. *Labour Elector,* November 9, 1889.

2. H. Llewellyn Smith and Vaughan Nash, *The Story of the Dockers' Strike,* London, 1889, p.8.

3. *Labour Elector,* August 24, 1889.

4. T. J. O'Keefe, *Rise and Progress of the National Amalgamated Labourers' Union of Great Britain and Ireland,* Cardiff, 1891, p.10.

5. *Cambria Daily Leader,* June 2, 1914.

6. Ibid, June 17, 1890.

7. Ibid.

8. Ibid, June 28, 1890.

9. Tom Mann and Ben Tillett, *The "New" Trades Unionism,* London, 1890, p.6.

10. *Dockers' Record,* March 1916; for further details on Wignall's career see Philip J. Leng, "James Wignall, Dockers' Leader and Labour M.P." in Joyce M. Bellamy and John Saville, *Dictionary of Labour Biography,* vol. 111, London 1976, pp. 205-6.

11. D. M. Richards, *The Honorary Freedom of the County Borough of Merthyr Tydfil Conferred upon Sir William Thomas Lewis,* Merthyr, 1908, p. 61.

12. *South Wales Daily News,* July 25, 1890.

13. *Timber Trades Journal,* November 26, 1892, p. 515.

14. *South Wales Daily News,* November 1, 1890.

15. *Royal Commission on Labour, 1892, C 6708-V, p. 237.*

16. Dockers' Union, *Minutes of Second Annual Congress,* London, 1891, p.5.

17. *South Wales Daily News,* February 3, 1891.

18. Ibid, February 10, 1891.

19. Ibid, February 18, 1891.

20. Ibid, March 2, 1891.

21. J. Havelock Wilson, *My Stormy Voyage Through Life,* London, 1925, p. 221.

22. *Cambria Daily Leader,* May 5, 1892.

23. Ibid, April 28, 1892.

24. *Western Daily Press,* November 26, 1892.

25. For further details on the history of trade unionism in Bristol see B. J. Atkinson, *The Bristol Labour Movement, 1868-1906,* D. Phil., Oxford,

1970; and P. J. Leng, *The Dock, Wharf, Riverside and General Labourers' Union in South Wales and Bristol, 1889-1921*, M. A. Kent., 1973.

26. Dockers' Union, *Annual Report,* London, 1893, p.12.

Chapter 2
Calm and Crescendo

On the Waterfront, 1894-1910

Although the Dockers' membership had decreased substantially between 1891 and 1893 (see **Appendix Two**), it subsequently remained fairly stable. In 1897 the union still had 10,000 members, for it retained strong support at hiring-centres where dockers had gained recognition from their employers. At these centres companies negotiated with union representatives, and several permanent boards of conciliation were established to resolve difficulties. Some specialised groups of workers such as coal trimmers even obtained wage increases, because trade gradually improved at the Welsh ports after 1894. Their officials, though, continued to discourage irresponsible strike action, as they did not want to offend waterfront firms and endanger the union's position. The employers, for their part, also behaved tolerantly towards the Dockers' Union. At various hiring-centres militant concerns had already broken the organisation and there was no need for them to reaffirm their position; elsewhere firms did not counter-attack because they did not wish to lose trade and incur much expense. Between 1894 and 1909 only one company tried to reduce the wages of the Dockers' members.

At Newport the attitude of the Alexandra Dock Company and other port employers enabled the Dockers' Union to survive, because they continued to recognise it and to bargain with its officials. The Dockers' two branches which consisted mainly of coal trimmers and tippers in fact grew during this period, and their memberships were 50% higher in 1899 than in 1894. They were strengthened to a large extent by the development of the coal trade, for their members were able to gain wage increases. The coal trimmers who had strong bargaining power especially benefited and obtained considerable "extras" (that is, supplementary charges for loading particular vessels). Yet strikes did not occur, because in return for recognition the union promised efficient and uninterrupted work. Wage disputes were settled by the Newport Coal Tipping and Trimming Conciliation Board which consisted of eight trimmers' representatives and eight representatives of the merchants, brokers and shipowners. Tillett's organisation was also strengthened after 1897 by the recruitment of groups of strategic importance such as iron-ore workers, ballast workers and deal runners. As a result, even though the union was virtually extinct at several ports such as London and Hull throughout the late 1890's, in 1899 it was stronger at Newport than it had been nine years previously.

Although coal trimmers at Newport stopped work for several days in March 1908 in protest against the hiring of Chinese sailors to load general cargo, good industrial relations were generally maintained at the port.

According to the **Dockers' Record**,

Newport demonstrates the strength of trades unionism in somewhat unique fashion. The port is well organised and well disciplined. Loyalty to the union and a willingness to follow the advice of officials are prominent features. As a result, it is very seldom a stoppage of work takes place; questions needing discussion being left for settlement between the officer and employers, which gives in almost every case complete satisfaction.[1]

Squabbling, nonetheless, continued between the Dockers' Union and the National Amalgamated Labourers' Union. At Newport the N.A.L.U. retained the support of the riverside workers, and it frequently tried to poach members from the Dockers. An agreement was made between the two organisations in 1905 to prevent men transferring from one union to the other unless they had clear cards and good reasons for changing, but the settlement was ignored by officials of the N.A.L.U. Dockers' leaders claimed that they still allowed men who had fallen behind with their subscriptions to the Dockers' Union to join their organisation,

> Our feeling is one of contempt for the leaders of a society who encourage poor weak-kneed knoblers to shelter themselves under the excuse of "transferred" knowing that they are indebted to us in large sums by way of contributions.[2]

At the port of Swansea the Dockers' Union also preserved its influence at various hiring-centres, and in 1894 was supported by patent fuel, tinshed and timber workers. The employers of these men recognised the Dockers' Union, allowed its branch representatives to make card checks at the calling-on stands, and did not try to undermine its position. Despite an increase in the number of outsiders at the docks after 1892 because of the decline of the tinplate industry, only one concern, the Graigola Patent Fuel Company, reduced wages. Following a decline in output, the company closed its works in March 1894 and announced that production would not restart until its three hundred employees had accepted a revised scale of wage-rates.

The workmen at the Graigola Works who belonged to the Dockers' Union were fully supported by their Executive Council and by the Swansea Trades and Labour Council, and were thus able to force the company to negotiate. At a meeting in late April Dockers' officials and the masters decided to resume operations at the works and to submit the issue to arbitration. The Mayor of Swansea, Colonel Pike, was selected as umpire, and his decision was announced several months later. He recommended that the existing tariff should remain in force and that the company should instead be relieved from its obligation to pay beer money to the men. This represented a decrease in wages of only a shilling a week in comparison with the substantial piece-work reduction which had been demanded by the employers. The men regretted the loss of their daily quota of ale, but they accepted the judgement and remained in the union.

Dockers' officials at Swansea, like those in Newport, subsequently emphasised conciliation, and were largely successful in preserving wage-rates and negotiating "extras". In particular, the election of Tom Merrells, the district secretary, to the Swansea Harbour Trust helped to minimise conflict on the waterfront. Merrells had access to the employers' accounts, and he always found the various concerns ready to examine the men's complaints. Nevertheless, he was still unable on occasions to prevent some members from striking unofficially, especially against the introduction of non-union labour.

In August, 1900, for instance, a dispute arose at Swansea docks because several labourers who had blacklegged during a strike in London a few months previously were hired. Over a hundred Swansea grain workers stopped work and announced that they would not resume until the "free" labourers were dismissed. But the employers refused to give way and obtained a hundred Shipping Federation labourers from Hull. The attitude of the employers led the strikers to ask their union for assistance, and Tillett himself became involved. He negotiated wage increases for the men, but could not prevent the conflict from affecting the nearby Weaver's flour mill where three mill-hands were dismissed for refusing to work overtime with the Federation labourers at the docks. At the mill workers bitterly opposed their company's decision, and after handing in their notices halted production. As they had recently become members of the Dockers' Union and followed union procedures, Tillett was obliged to declare the strike official and to play a vigorous part.

Even though he still preferred to solve disputes by conciliation, the Dockers' Secretary knew that harmony would not prevail until the firm recognised his organisation. He therefore arranged the picketing of every shop in Swansea where Weaver's flour was sold, and sent organisers to Devon to prevent the concern from obtaining "scab" labourers there. As he explained,

> That man should have been born in Nero's time, this little Swansea nabob, this poor deluded creature must be taught a lesson; must be made to realise that that day had gone by when labour was to be trodden upon.[3]

Tillett, on the other hand, did not approve of the violent behaviour of some of the strikers who protested against the company employing blacklegs. On 28th August a large crowd of men and their wives attacked the mill, threw stones at the windows, and battered down the gates. However, no further violence occurred, for the directors capitulated the next day and recognised the men's leaders. The question of increased wages was also discussed, and all the regular workers were reinstated.

Despite the Dockers' success, its Swansea officials did not pursue militant policies but preferred to settle disputes with their employers by conciliation. Between 1900 and 1910 they negotiated many wage improvements: at the Atlantic, Graigola and Pacific Patent Fuel Works wage-rates were increased by 22½% between 1901 and 1908; at the port the tariff for general dock labourers was revised in 1901 and 1907. Due to these settlements and a growth of trade the Dockers' membership increased, and in 1909 contributions in the district were over three times the amount for 1898. The union's influence continued to be based chiefly around the timber workers, tinshed men and patent fuel workers whose branches were recognised by their employers, but it also tried to enforce its ticket in other parts of the port. Its action again led to conflict with the National Amalgamated Labourers' Union, and a small dispute was fought between the two organisations at Weaver's grain warehouse in January 1908 over the monopoly of work issue.

On the Cardiff waterfront, though, Tillett's union was unable to make such progress because of the opposition of large firms, especially the Cardiff Railway Company. This concern, which had changed its name from the Bute Docks Company in 1894 for commercial reasons, still refused to recognise its officials and was prepared to negotiate only with the port workers themselves. As a result of the company's attitude the Dockers' Union was moribund between January 1895-June 1897. However, in July 1897 following a growth of the timber trade it intervened in a dispute between the Cardiff deal runners and the timber merchants. Even though the men were not members, the union's leaders gave financial support and sent the national organisers, Harry Orbell and James Wignall, to the district. They advised the 650 workers who had struck for an increase of 1/6d. per day and two pints of beer to return to the yards while they attempted to negotiate with the timber merchants. Yet the employers proved to be uncompromising, and 500 men again left work a week later. The master stevedores immediately awarded a substantial wage increase, but the larger firms imported blackleg labour from Hull to crush the strike. These concerns refused to meet union officials, and William Riley, a prominent timber merchant, announced that the workmen were welcome to return on the old terms provided they agreed to work alongside the "free" labourers. Although the "free" labourers themselves struck over a wage claim, the deal runners hired by large firms were eventually forced to accept their employers' terms and resumed work in August. During the dispute membership of the Dockers' local branch had expanded to its highest level since 1892, but this defeat caused its decline and within several months the union was again moribund on the Cardiff waterfront.

Nonetheless, the organisation did subsequently manage to enrol workers employed by smaller Cardiff concerns, and local representatives eventually raised enough support to start a branch of iron-ore labourers in 1901. In addition, a branch of pitwood workers was formed in 1904 as a result of the activities of George Lock, and its members gained wage advances and recognition from several contractors. A branch of dry dock workers was also established in 1907, but union leaders failed to regain the support of the coal trimmers who remained in their own craft society and the tippers who were re-organised in 1898 by the Amalgamated Society of Railway Servants. The inability of Dockers' officials to recruit workers of strategic importance retarded the union's development at the port for it was impossible to halt work there: in 1909 its membership in Cardiff was less than a third of that at Newport.

The Dockers' Union, however, made considerable progress at Barry Dock after 1906 and was recognised by the dock company and port employers. Frederick Rogers, the union's district officer, enrolled 1200 workers and formed five branches before 1908. Pitwood workers, riggers, ballast workers, hobblers, flour millmen and dry dock workers joined, but Rogers could not persuade the local coal trimmers who were members of the Cardiff, Penarth and Barry Coal Trimmers to affiliate. At Port Talbot, though, Dockers' officials did succeed in recruiting the coal trimmers at the docks, for the Cardiff Coal Trimmers' Association was uninterested in widening its influence.

The progress of the Dockers' Union after 1889, thus, differed from that of the Labour Protection League, a union of port workers formed in London in 1872. Whereas the Labour Protection League collapsed following a counter-attack by employers, the Dockers' Union remained in existence because it spread to the provinces and recruited employees of companies which were prepared to recognise its leaders. Yet Tillett's organisation, as we have seen, was itself affected by the attitude of employing concerns. In the early 1890's London and Hull were its main strongholds, but they later suffered considerable set-backs at the hands of the shipowners and dock companies. In South Wales and Bristol, on the other hand, a number of employers allowed it to survive, and its strength was largely concentrated there between 1894 and 1900.

The National Amalgamated Labourers' Union also survived the employers' counter-attack between 1891-93. Although none of its records for the period 1891-1914 seem to have been retained, *Annual Reports on Trade Unions* state that its membership was:

Annual Membership of the National Amalgamated Labourers' Union between 1892-1910

Year	Total number of members	Year	Total number of members
1892	3914	1901	3627
1893	3015	1902	3189
1894	2871	1903	3058
1895	2823	1904	3174
1896	3692	1905	2085
1897	3335	1906	2200
1898	3073	1907	3154
1899	3695	1908	3195
1900	3505	1909	3166
		1910	3549

Table 3

Newspapers also show that the N.A.L.U.'s members were not very militant on the waterfront during these years. Like the Dockers' rank and file they had probably learned much from their heavy defeats by the employers. Furthermore, the Dockers, and possibly the N.A.L.U., was largely composed of men who had certain skills and who, because of their strong bargaining power, were able to negotiate wage increases without using strike action. It was in fact mainly non-unionists who were involved in the few stoppages that occurred during this period. Benefiting from improvements in trade such as in 1897 and 1900 unorganised dockers, as we have described, vigorously demanded wage increases. But they did not return to the union until the trade boom of 1911, for they realised that the conciliatory policies of the Dockers' leaders were of little benefit to them.

The recruitment of tinplate workers, 1892-1910.

The decline of the Dockers' Union in South Wales after 1891 was not confined to the waterfront. Following the collapse of the coal tippers' strike in March 1891, the Cardiff gasworkers left the union and by 1894 the Swansea copper workers had also withdrawn. The loss of these members weakened the organisation: its funds decreased and it missed the benefit of having their levies and regular contributions when strikes affected the waterside. Consequently, though industrial unrest decreased at the ports after 1894, Dockers' officials realised that the recruitment of other strategic groups was essential. Thus, when a local society of tinplate workers, the South Wales, Monmouthshire and Gloucestershire Tinplate Association, was dissolved in 1899, they made a determined effort to enrol its members.

Before the recruitment of the tinplate workers is discussed, it is necessary to explain the failure of Tillett's organisation to retain the copper workers. Over 1600 copper workers from Taibach, Skewen, Morfa and Port Talbot had joined the union in 1890, but many left in 1892 as they received inadequate support from its representatives during strikes at their plants. In 1894 the remainder also left to form their own association with local smelter and chemical workers, because Dockers' leaders refused to recognise them as a skilled body of mechanics and because they had been insufficiently represented in the union. They had had branch delegates, but the district official at Swansea was a dock worker who was mainly concerned with developments on the waterfront.

The loss of the copper workers contributed to the decline of membership contributions at Swansea which fell by over 80% between 1890 and 1896. However, the Dockers' Union was strengthened by its recruitment of a large number of tinplate workers after their association collapsed in January 1899. The Tinplate Workers' Union which had been formed in 1887 was dissolved chiefly because of its failure to protect wages and conditions. Following the introduction of the McKinley Tariff Act by the American Republican Party in July 1891 which considerably increased the duty on tinplate, tinplate production declined and unemployment increased in South Wales. In April 1896 12,650 tinplate workers out of a total labour force of approximately 26,000 were redundant. The decline in production led the employers to demand wage reductions, and they were largely successful because the union was unable to resist strongly in these adverse conditions. Moreover, as the tinplate manufacturers' society was dissolved in 1896, wages were not reduced uniformly. Although a standard wage list, the "1874 list", existed for the industry, the masters acted individually and made agreements with their own men and not with the union. The leaders of the Tinplate Workers' Union tried to regain a uniform wage-scale in 1897 by proposing that wage-rates should be fixed at a level which represented a reduction of 15% on the "1874 list", but their decision alienated the most loyal members, the Briton Ferry workers, who objected and left the organisation. Lacking support, finances and the recognition of many employers, the union was forced to dissolve.

Other factors also contributed to its collapse. It was, for instance, as unsuccessful in its effort to restrict output as it was in maintaining wage-rates. The union had attempted to limit production per man shift to the making of thirty-six boxes, but it was forced to abandon this restriction in Llanelly, Briton Ferry and other areas before 1896. Its failure led members in these districts to leave the organisation and to join the Gasworkers' Union. The Tinplate Workers' Union was also much weakened after 1890 by disagreements between workers in the tinhouses and those in the mills over the sale of blackplate (that is, untinned sheets) to America. Whereas the millmen who produced this material benefited from the export of their product, the tinhousemen claimed that the sale of blackplate was helping to establish tinplate production in the United States and they tried to prevent its manufacture. Relations between these two groups over this issue and other difficulties became so embittered that when the union collapsed they decided to join different organisations.

The Tinplate Workers' Union ceased to exist on 14th January, 1899, when a conference of delegates at Swansea formally dissolved the union and decided by 2,030 votes to 565 to form separate societies for the tinhousemen and the millmen. Although this decision affected the development of unionism in the industry, the number of tinhousemen represented at the meeting was small. Most of them were absent because of their lack of interest; some in fact had already joined the Dockers' Union. Despite the existence of the Tinplate Workers' Union, Tillett's organisation had formed a branch at Cwmfelin during the winter months of 1898.

Tillett was later criticised for poaching, but there was little evidence to link his officials with the collapse of the Tinplate Workers' Union. Its dissolution put an end to such allegations, and led to considerable competition amongst unions which were anxious to increase their ranks by recruiting its members. During the following months the millmen were enrolled by the British Steel Smelters' Association led by John Hodge and the newly formed Tin and Sheet Millmen's Association; the tinhousemen were organised by the Dockers, the Gasworkers and the Welsh Artisans' Union which had been founded in 1888 by John Edwards.

In spite of the financial weakness of the Dockers' Union during the late 1890's, it was an unusual development for its officials to become interested in the recruitment of the tinplate workers. In the first place, Tillett's union was a general labourers' organisation; the tinplate workers, on the other hand, were skilled, and only workmen from the tinplate industry had been allowed to join the Tinplate Workers' Association. Indeed, the process workers, who were directly involved with the manufacture of tinplate in the mill or in the tinhouse, were recruited according to skill and seniority. New entrants to the industry initially began work as cold-roll boy, list boy or grease boy, and were then promoted in either the mill or the tinhouse when a vacancy occurred. Within the mill promotion was from behinder to furnacemen, then to doubler, and finally to rollerman or to shearer; in the tinhouse, promotion was from list-boy to riser, then to wash man, to tinman, and finally to assorter. Workers learned their next job by carefully watching those with whom they were working and then by practice. In the second place, whereas the Dockers' Union was managed on a centralised basis, some tinplate workmen favoured local autonomy. Even though the Tinplate Workers' Association had had a centralised constitution, its leaders had frequently been unable to control their rank and file. At Llanelly and Morriston, for instance, in 1892 tinplate workers had discussed secession from the union because of the payment of relief to unemployed members.

In spite of a determined recruitment campaign by Will Thorne, the Gasworkers' Secretary, in the tinplate district of West Wales during the first half of 1899, most tinhousemen joined the Dockers' Union. In June 1899 Tillett's organisation claimed over 2,500 members and had twenty-four new branches in the Swansea district. Its success was largely due to its prominence in the area, for it had local officials such as James Wignall who were in the vicinity at the time of the collapse of the Tinplate Workers' Union and who played an active role. Tillett's oratorical powers also won support for the Dockers' Union, especially as he was a more convincing speaker than Thorne. In addition the Dockers' Union set up a separate "emergency fund" to provide friendly benefits to tinplate workers, and demanded a general improvement in wage-rates.

Tillett also tried to establish a new wage structure for the industry. At a Joint Conference which was held between representatives of the companies and unions at Swansea in March 1899 he recommended,

> An alliance be established between the employers and workers for the purpose of securing fair profits and good wages compatible with the competitive interests of the trade[4]

and suggested that a wages board consisting of an equal number of employers and workmen should be formed in order that questions of pay, hours and conditions of labour could be amicably agreed. This board would establish a uniform rate of payment for the industry and prevent bargaining between individual firms and workmen by setting up a sliding scale of wages. Tillett also wanted to regulate prices in order to safeguard the men's employment and the profits of the companies. He proposed that the men would not work for any manufacturer who sold tinplates at a reduced price, and in return the employers would not employ non-unionists. Tillett's scheme was intended to ensure the future prosperity of both the tinplate companies and their workmen, and to minimise industrial conflict in the industry.

These recommendations which were based largely upon a scheme adopted by the brass bedstead industry received a mixed reception from the tinplate companies. A number of employers believed that the methods adopted by the brass bedstead industry were irrelevant to the tinplate industry; others were probably more opposed to the proposed increase of wages. At a conference held at Swansea in March 1899 to hear Mr. E. J. Smith, the Chairman of the Brass Bedstead and Metal Trade Alliance, only 82 out of 318 mills at work were represented. Nevertheless, the employers who attended this meeting decided to form a committee to carefully consider the scheme. Although it was later resolved not to accept Tillett's proposals, most tinplate companies approved the re-establishment of an employers' association, because the workers had become members of large national unions and because the export of tinplates to Europe increased in 1899. As one employer stressed, "Never before have tinplate employers so felt the need of co-operation."[5]

The companies formed their association, the Welsh Plate and Sheet Manufacturers' Association, in May 1899. It was not based upon the scheme supported by Tillett, but was established with the object of protecting its members, maintaining uniform wage rates and creating a conciliation board. Tillett's suggestions to fix the standard selling price of tinplates and to set up a permanent alliance between employers and workmen were rejected because they were considered to be too far-reaching. Yet most tinplate companies co-operated with the unions as they wanted to resuscitate the industry, and a conciliation board was set up and met at Swansea for the first time in June 1899. Representatives of the firms, the Dockers', Gasworkers', Steel Smelters', and the Tin and Sheet Millmen's Unions were present at this meeting and made an important agreement. Wage-rates throughout the industry, it was decided, were to be 10% below the "1874 list" for August and September 1899, and the list was to be completely restored on 1st October and to remain in force until 31st March, 1900. In order to prevent industrial strife in the tinplate industry, the members of the Conciliation Board also decided to make annual wage agreements which would raise or lower wages according to the level of trade, and to settle disputes by a Joint Committee consisting of three elected representatives from each side. If this Committee was unable to reach a settlement, the matter was to be referred to an independant arbitrator. However, the Joint Committee itself was successful in most cases: between 1907 and 1910 it settled 84 disputes and passed only three to arbitration.

This machinery generally worked well, but the Conciliation Board was unable to equalise wages and hours throughout the trade because it did not immediately gain the full co-operation of unions and employers. The Welsh Artisans' Union did not join until 1909, and about 20% of the tinplate mills remained unaffiliated as late as 1912. The introduction of uniform conditions in the industry was also obstructed by the unions who quarrelled amongst themselves. A demarcation agreement was made between Hodge's Steel Smelters' Union and Tillett shortly after the collapse of the Tinplate Workers' Union, but great rivalry existed between them and Phillips, the Secretary of the Tin and Sheet Millmen's Union, who jealously opposed their enrollment of tinplate workers. Relations became so strained that a Wages and Disputes Board which the unions set up in 1901 to give them a common policy at Conciliation Board meetings broke up in 1904 because of a disagreement between the tinhousemen and the millmen.

The Conciliation Board also found it difficult at first to resolve differences between employers and workmen over wages. Its problems began as early as April 1900 when the unions submitted a request to the Board for an increase in wage-rates of 15%. Their leaders believed that the proposal was justified, because the price of tinplates was abnormally high at the time and the steel workers had already received increases of $17\frac{1}{2}\%$; yet firms were not convinced that such an increase was warranted. A bitter confrontation over the issue was prevented only by the disunity of the unions. Hodge's members handed in their notices, but Tillett and Phillips were not prepared to risk weakening the Conciliation Board and refused to support a strike. Consequently the Steel Smelters' Union was forced to back down and to accept the employers' terms that the "1874 list" should remain in force until June 1901.

Despite some changes, this list was renewed in June 1901 and again in July 1902, though union representatives were not completely satisfied nor were the workers. Llanelly firemen who belonged to the Gasworkers' Union struck between 29th September and 6th October, 1902 over the length of shifts. Their demands were examined by a Joint Committee of the Conciliation Board and were approved. A more serious situation developed over the issue of whether tinplate workers should be paid by the area or by the weight of the tinplates they produced. The Steel Smelters' Union pressed for the basis of payment to be altered from weight to area, and in June 1903 the members of the Conciliation Board debated the matter. An agreement was made, but it was later objected to by members of the Steel Smelters' Union. Their opposition led the employers to close their works and to lock out over 14,000 workers in September 1903. Fortunately for the industry the lock-out ended a week later, and the question was submitted to a Board of Trade arbitrator, Sir K. E. Digby. Digby's award which was issued in January 1904 favoured the companies but was accepted by the unions.

Even though Tillett had demanded wage increases in 1899 in order to win members, he played an insignificant part during these disputes. He tried in fact to prevent conflict, and the strikes were caused by members of other unions. As the Dockers had gained a large tinplate membership, Tillett saw little need to press wage demands and subsequently did little to mar industrial relations in the industry. Between 1904 and 1910 the "1874 list" was renewed at each annual meeting, and only slight modifications were made. His organisation made requests for weekly instead of monthly payments and for wage increases, but these were not put forward forcefully. Tillett believed that it was better to settle disputes by negotiation rather than by strike action:

It is best for both employers and employed to haggle for a month or months when machinery is running and trade maintained than when lockout, strike or stoppage paralyses industry and losses and ruin result.[6]

Although exports of tinplates increased from 256,373 tons in 1899 to 482,981 tons in 1910 as a result of the growth of European markets, strike action was never threatened by the Dockers' Union to advance its members' wages.

In spite of the attitude of Dockers' officials, the tinplate workers remained loyal to the union, for they were paid friendly benefits and were impressed by its past achievements, particularly the great victory on the Thames in 1889. Furthermore, though the Dockers' leaders did not press the men's demands, at least they preserved the "1874 list". Even if it was chiefly the favourable economic conditions which helped them to do this, they diꞓ keep wage-rates at this level for longer than the Tinplate Workers' Union had done. In 1902 restrictions on output were also abandoned, and the wages of tinplate workers increased as their production per shift grew. Average earnings for full-time workers in 1906 were:

Average earnings for full-time tinplate workers of South Wales, Monmouthshire and Gloucestershire in 1906[7].

Workers (of and above 20 years of age) in the tinplate industry	Average earnings for full time	
	s.	d.
Furnacemen working at piece-rate	47	3
Rollers working at piece-rate	62	10
Doublers working at piece-rate	50	9
Behinders working at piece-rate	26	9
Shearers working at piece-rate	61	3
Annealers working at piece-rate	41	11
Tinmen working at piece-rate	43	6
Assorters working at piece-rate	50	5
Boxers working at piece-rate	45	1
General labourers working at day-rate	22	9

Table 4

As wages stayed at a relatively high level in the industry, the membership of Tillett's union increased, and it formed a separate tinplate district in West Wales in 1908. The tinplate workers' branches were extremely important to the union, as their combined annual income soon became greater than those of other districts in the organisation (see Appendix Two). Whereas the tinplate workers contributed over £1,500 to the central fund in 1908, the combined incomes of the London and Hull areas amounted to only £155. The subscriptions received from the tinplate district compensated for the weakness of these centres which had declined because of the employers' counter-attack in the early 1890's, and helped to finance the union's dispute pay on the waterfront.

The Dockers' Union also tried to recruit workers from other industries after 1900. Its officials persuaded the copper workers to rejoin, and they formed the basis of a new district established at Port Talbot in 1908. Branches were opened at Skewen, Taibach, Briton Ferry and Morfa, and wage increases were negotiated. However, because of rivalry between the copper firms, Tillett was unable to create a conciliation board for the industry. The union also enrolled galvanizers in various Monmouthshire towns, chemical workers in Briton Ferry, corporation workmen in Swansea, and sheet metal workers at the works of John Lysaght in Newport; but after a lock-out in December 1904 its two Lysaght's branches were dissolved.

Although some members of the old Tinplate Workers' Union had demanded greater local autonomy, this issue never threatened to weaken the Dockers' Union. The tinplate workers had a district secretary and three representatives on the Executive Council in 1910, and they ensured that the men's views were well heard. On the other hand, the leaders of the union and the tinplate workers did disagree over their political affiliations. In February 1900 the Dockers' Union helped to form the Labour Representation Committee, and its officials later encouraged the establishment of constituency parties in towns such as Newport and Swansea and assisted working-class candidates standing at parliamentary elections. At Swansea, where several dock workers sat on the Council, local support was felt to be so strong that Ben Tillett was invited to stand as Labour candidate in the Swansea Town Parliamentary Election in January 1910. His candidature, nonetheless, was strongly opposed by many tinplate workers who backed the Liberal Party's free trade policies, as they had suffered considerably from the effects of the McKinley Tariff. During the election campaign they criticised Tillett for forcing a three-cornered fight in the constituency to the disadvantage of the Liberal candidate, for disagreeing with Lloyd George's budget, and for holding political meetings on a Sunday. According to one prominent tinplate representative,

> The workers of Wales were men of more deeply religious convictions than men of the same class in England. Fancy Mr. Tillett holding two political meetings on the Sunday![8]

The tinplate workers were so hostile to Tillett's candidature that they threatened to leave his union unless he pulled out of the election. Tillett stubbornly ignored their threats and was heavily defeated by the Liberal candidate, Alfred Mond, who polled over four times as many votes; but his defeat pacified the men and they remained members.

The Houlder dispute of 1910

Between 1893 and 1910 the Dockers' Union had survived on the waterfront in South Wales largely because of the unbelligerence of various local concerns, and only one attempt had been made by employers to reduce its members' wages. The long period of acquiescence, however, was shattered in May 1910 when a determined effort was made by Houlder Brothers, a national shipping company, to alter its method of payment at the Alexandra Dock, Newport, where it shipped general cargoes. Houlders tried to revert from piece-work to the day-wage system of payment, but the proposed change was strongly opposed by members of the Dockers' Union and the N.A.L.U. who were affected. It was to the men's advantage to keep the existing system: with piece-work they could increase their wages considerably by working quickly, but on a day-wage basis they would be paid only a fixed wage. Employment was also less casual under piece-work: on the day-wage system a man could be replaced after four hours, but a labourer on piece-work was guaranteed employment until the work on a particular ship was completed. Nonetheless, Houlders were determined to make this change because they had discovered that many of their cargoes had been damaged by dockers working at speed, and they realised that it would reduce their wage-bill. The company was a prominent member of the Shipping Federation and was confident that it would succeed, but it considerably underestimated the men's resistance. The port workers refused to compromise, ignored their union officials who favoured arbitration, and supported local militants who ordered the boycotting of Houlders' ships.

The dispute began on 14th May, 1910 when the shipowners' vessel, *Indian Transport,* arrived at the port. Houlders announced that the ship was to be loaded by men hired on the day-wage system, but the general cargo labourers refused to stow its cargo until they were promised piece-work rates of payment. Although only a hundred workmen were affected by the proposed change, they were backed by other dockers who feared that an alteration in the system of payment would lead to a reduction of wages and a lengthening of working hours throughout the port. According to Alfred Cox, a prominent leader of the general cargo workers,

> They did not wish to bring the work to the low and degrading level it occupied in other large seaports. Under the old system, they worked the whole time that the ship was loading. If, however, the day-work system was brought into operation, the men would have no guarantee of being employed after the first day of loading. They would be paid daily and others might be taken on in their place on the following day. That would be the means of attracting a larger number of men to the docks than were actually required with the result that work would be more irregular.[9]

But Houlders refused to compromise; they applied to the Shipping Federation for substitutes, and fifty two men were sent by train from London several days later. It was the first time at Newport docks that blackleg labour had been imported on such a scale.

The Newport dockers were angered by the arrival of the "free" labourers in the town, and they unofficially declared a general strike at the docks on 18th May. Three hundred men also converged upon the *Indian Transport* where the London labourers were based, and when several of the blacklegs came ashore to move cranes violence broke out. One of the strikers, Edward O'Neill screamed abusively, "You bloody bastards, you bloody cows, you f.....g whores", and turning to the crowd asked, "Are we going to let them take the bread out of our mouths? Let us go for them."[10] The dockers then rushed towards the blacklegs, beat them up on the quay, and stoned the ship. Several hours later the crowd had increased to about a thousand, and another effort was made to take over the vessel. A number of strikers shouted, "Rush the gangway, lower the cranes, and get some tubs, we must get aboard and get the buggers out of it",[11] and the dockers, many of whom brandished sticks and lumps of iron ore, again tried to climb aboard. This attempt was also unsuccessful, but two of the men's local union representatives, John O'Leary and John Twomey, were invited aboard by the captain to address the Federation men, and they offered to pay their fares back to London and to guarantee them protection if they left the ship immediately. Their proposal was accepted, and the "free" labourers were escorted to Newport railway station by the dockers and put on the London train.

The next day the strikers organised a procession of two thousand men through Newport led by a drum and fife band to gain the sympathy of workers in the town. Except for the damage caused by a drunken docker who staggered from the procession and fell through a plate glass shop window, the event passed without incident. A serious effort, moreover, was made by Henry Seer, the Dockers' district secretary, and union representatives to settle the issue. Unlike militants such as Alf Cox and George Jackson, a local seamen's leader, they were determined to prevent the dispute from becoming a major conflict throughout the Bristol Channel. The Dockers' officials were assisted by the Mayor of Newport who also wished to achieve a settlement quickly. He attended a meeting several days later between the unionists and John Macaulay, the Manager of the Alexandra Docks Company, who represented Houlder Brothers. At this discussion it was agreed that work would be resumed at the docks under the old conditions until the question of wages at the port was finally decided by arbitration.

Yet the settlement was not accepted by Messrs. Houlder who argued that Macaulay was not authorised to act for them. They refused to proceed with the loading of their ship on the old terms and would not allow the issue to be resolved by arbitration. The company also announced that imported labour brought by the Shipping Federation's depot ship, *Lady Jocelyn,* would unload the vessel. As a private concern Houlder Brothers was certainly under the impression that troops, extra police and gun-boats would be sent to the town to protect these workmen. Frank Houlder argued,

In the Argentine they managed these things better; they would send artillery and machine guns, and give proper protection to their subjects. He claimed his rights as a British citizen, and said the Government must give him the protection to which he was entitled by law.[12]

Nevertheless, the local authorities refused to provide protection for Houlders' blacklegs, and they were supported by the Board of Trade and the Home Office. Government representatives such as Sydney Buxton, the President of the Board of Trade, and Sir Edward Troup believed that the arrival of "free" labour would lead to further bloodshed. Troup, too, had little sympathy with Houlders: in a letter to Winston Churchill he remarked that, "If Mr. Houlder bullied his stevedores as he tried to bully me, it is no wonder there was a strike!"[13] Lacking the necessary assurances, Houlders had little alternative but to accept arbitration.

The arbitration proceedings were held at London and were judged by a Board of Trade representative, Sir David Harrel. Evidence was chiefly supplied by the union and the shipowners, but Newport firms also testified and refused to support a change in the method of payment. The piece-work system had been the custom at the port for forty years, and the dock company and the stevedores believed that the men would not make so much effort working for day-wages. They had had little trouble from the unions since 1889 and realised that the dispute was mainly the responsibility of Houlder Brothers. Harrel, however, decided in favour of the shipowners and declared that employers at the port of Newport could hire men either at piece-work rates or at the day-wage of eight shillings. The Dockers' Union leaders were disappointed by the award but accepted it, for Tillett argued that they must abide by their compacts. The general cargo workers at Newport, on the other hand, refused to accept this decision, overwhelmingly rejected Tillett's proposal that they should give the award a trial, and declined to load the *Indian Transport* for day-work wages. The men were refused strike pay, but were helped by Alf Cox who had become very prominent during the strike.

Alf Cox was a Newport-born man who had been employed at the Alexandra Docks for much of his working life. He had fought in the Boer War, was a good orator, and was an avid reader of Marx. Although he was a member of the Dockers' Union, he was determined not to accept the arbitration award and started a fund to help his fellow cargo workers. His fervour was increased at this time by his discovery of syndicalism, a philosophy which had also been accepted by Tom Mann during his experiences in Australia between 1902 and 1910. Mann had found that the Australian worker had benefited little from political labour parties and compulsory arbitration acts, and argued in his pamphlet, *The Way to Win*, which was published in 1909, "Reliance upon parliamentary action would never bring freedom".[14] Instead, Mann believed that the salvation of the working-class could be achieved only by means of the trade union movement. But he realised that trade unions would have to lose much of their sectional character, and advocated their merger to form one union only for each industry. Mann, in addition, advised unionists not to make long-term wage agreements with their employers but to strike at every opportunity. Each dispute, he believed, would be a preparation for a final upheaval when the workers of the country would strike unitedly and force Parliament to resign. The trade union movement would take control of the country's government, and administration would be carried out by national, district and local unionist bodies. Capitalism would be abolished and the exploitation of the working-class would be ended, because individuals would gain the full fruits of their labour.

Although Mann had accepted these theories before his return to England in May 1910, his beliefs were firmly established by a subsequent visit to France. With Guy Bowman who was an active socialist in London he travelled to Paris to study the development of the Confédération Général du Travail, a French organisation. Following their arrival back in London, they began to spread the theory of syndicalism and published a monthly pamphlet called *The Industrial Syndicalist.* Mann also gave many addresses in various parts of the country, and in June 1910 he arrived in South Wales and spoke at Newport, Cardiff, Penarth, Barry, Port Talbot and Swansea. His campaign attracted much attention, for it was closely connected with the wave of industrial unrest which was developing in many industries. Only two weeks after Mann's visit to the Principality, Cuthbert Laws, the General Manager of the Shipping Federation, remarked that, "In all the South Wales ports, socialistic trade unionism has gained a very great ascendancy."[15] Yet Laws considerably overestimated the influence of syndicalism. Even though Mann influenced Alf Cox (Cox became known locally as "Tom Mann the Second"), Cox's brother George, George Jackson, and a number of dock labourers and seamen in South Wales, his ideas were not as widely held as the shipowners believed and he had not caused the Houlder dispute. Most of the rank and file of the Dockers' Union continued to be concerned with gaining higher wages and were not interested in overthrowing capitalism.

Despite this, Alf Cox was strongly supported by Newport cargo workers who realised that, if they were to prevent Houlders imposing lower wages upon them, it would be due to his leadership and not to the less militant policies of Tillett's Executive Council. They followed his instructions and continued to refuse to handle any goods belonging to Houlders. The firm was forced to use Shipping Federation labourers who were lodged aboard the depot ship, *Lady Jocelyn,* in the Bristol Channel. The shipping company claimed that the Federation's labourers were more energetic and less vulgar than the Newport men, but their employment was undoubtedly more expensive because it began to divert some of its ships to Bristol. As Bristol was chiefly a day-work port the company did not anticipate any resistance. Houlders, however, underestimated the strength of the port workers' organisation, for their first ship to arrive at Avonmouth was "blacked" by twenty dock labourers who were acting in sympathy with the Newport men. The dockers asked the shipowners to send their vessel, *Natal Transport,* to Newport, but the company refused and threatened to import "free" labour. As a result the dispute was extended, and over a thousand dock workers at Avonmouth left work on 22nd June. William Gorman, the Dockers' district secretary at Bristol, urged them to return to work, but the men remained united. Their militancy provided an opportunity for Alf Cox to take advantage of the situation. He travelled to Bristol, spoke at a mass meeting of the strikers on the waterfront, and advised the crippling of Houlder Brothers, "the tools of the Federation",[16] recommending that their ships should be allowed to rot in the dock. But Cox also suggested that the men should return to work on every vessel except the *Natal Transport,* because he knew that they would not obtain strike pay from the union. Even though Gorman urged his members to honour existing agreements and to work on all ships at the port, the men accepted Cox's proposal.

At Bristol the strike over Houlders' ship was settled three days later, but on 12th July port workers at Avonmouth struck unofficially again because of the employment of three foremen who had continued working during the first dispute. Alf Cox returned to Bristol and told the Bristol dockers that they would be able to gain the sympathy of workers throughout the Bristol Channel ports. Yet, except for a one day strike in Newport, the dispute was confined to Bristol and a settlement was negotiated two weeks later by union officials. At Bristol the men abided by this agreement, and good industrial relations were restored; but at Newport the port workers refused to compromise, because they believed that acceptance of Harrel's award would mean a victory for "free" labour. Instead they continued to hold out against loading Houlders' ships, and rallied behind Cox and George Jackson.

At Newport, local syndicalists remained in the forefront of activities on the waterfront. Only a year later a boom in trade developed; from defending the men's position against Houlders they switched to demand an improvement in wages and conditions. In July 1911 industrial conflict broke out at Newport docks and throughout the South Wales ports, and it was encouraged by the militants. In these stoppages, however, syndicalist objectives were not emphasised by more than a few of the strikers. As in the Houlder issue, militant trade unionists were thanked by the men not for their revolutionary outbursts but for their help in organising disputes and promoting wage demands.

52

NOTES

1. *Dockers' Record,* February 1901, p.2.
2. Ibid, November, 1906, p.3.
3. *Cambria Daily Leader,* August 20, 1900.
4. *South Wales Daily News,* March 22, 1899.
5. Ibid, April 20, 1899.
6. Ibid, May 3, 1900.
7. *Report of an Enquiry by the Board of Trade into the Earnings and Hours of Labour of Workpeople in the United Kingdom,* 1911, Cd. 5814, p.56.
8. *South Wales Daily News,* January 10, 1910.
9. Ibid, May 20, 1910.
10. Newport Dock Dispute, 1910, Houlder Brothers Limited v. Newport Corporation, Minutes of Arbitration, vol. 5, p.19.
11. Ibid, p.22.
12. Randolph S. Churchill, *Winston S. Churchill,* London, 1969, Volume II, Companion Part II, pp. 1172-3.
13. Ibid, p.1171.
14. Tom Mann, *Tom Mann's Memoirs,* London, 1923, p.239.
15. *South Wales Daily News,* June 25, 1910.
16. *Western Daily Press,* June 23, 1910.

Chapter 3
Strikers, Blacklegs and Bullies

The 1911 dock strikes

As in 1889 the development of industrial unrest on the waterfront arose to a large extent from the growth of trade. Influenced by increased business at the Bristol Channel ports (for example, coal exports at Newport rose from approximately 3.80 million tons in 1910 to 4.31 million tons in 1911, and at Swansea from 2.85 million tons to 3.08 million tons), a decline in unemployment and rising prices, the port workers demanded wage advances. Men, of course, could more readily defy their employers when the supply of potential "blacklegs" was at its lowest. They were also encouraged by a national dispute between the National Sailors' and Firemen's Union and the Shipping Federation. In July 1910 the Seamen's Union had demanded the formation of a national conciliation board, a uniform scale of wages for all ports and control of hiring procedures; but the employers had rejected its demands, and a national strike was eventually declared on 14th June, 1911.

The Seamen's leaders asked the Dockers, the National Amalgamated Labourers' Union and other organisations connected with the carrying trades for support, for along with their representatives they had set up the National Transport Workers' Federation in November 1910 to reduce sectionalism and to strengthen the position of workers in the transport industry. At first, though, members of the National Transport Workers' Federation did not favour strike action; the Dockers in particular had suffered serious defeats in the past by assisting the Seamen's Union against the Shipping Federation. Thus, when dockers struck at Swansea on 23rd June in support of the seamen, Tillett ordered an immediate return to work. However, because port workers elsewhere decided to back the seamen with militant action, the attitude of the National Transport Workers' Federation altered. According to John Twomey, the Secretary of the National Amalgamated Labourers' Union,

> The feeling of many of the executive (i.e. N.T.W.F.) is that since trouble is being forced upon the unions the best thing is to endeavour to get it over as soon as possible.[1]

Despite this change of policy, the dock strikes in South Wales in July were not officially declared. While the leaders of the Dockers' Union were involved in negotiations in London with the Port of London Authority, shipowners and wharfingers, South Wales dockers struck suddenly for increased wages. They were influenced to some extent by local militants such as George Jackson, and by Madame Sorgue, a prominent French syndicalist, who toured the area in June and spoke at several meetings on behalf of the seamen. Yet it seems that the men were largely persuaded to leave work by the militancy of Captain Edward Tupper, the South Wales organiser of the Seamen's Union. Tupper was a good orator and was very flamboyant. At his union meetings in Bute Street, Cardiff, he wore a morning coat and a silk top hat, drank large quantities of 'Bass', and frequently challenged Shipping Federation toughs and employers to box against him at the Neptune Park,

Cardiff. On 17th July Tupper issued a challenge to Mr. E. Handcock, a Cardiff tug-boat owner, to fight him for £50, and at the head of a large procession he marched to Handcock's office. The demonstration got out of hand, and coal and jack-knives were thrown through the company's windows. Tupper was arrested, served with sixteen summonses, and appeared at the City Hall the next day.

His presence in court had a considerable effect upon industrial relations at Cardiff. Local members of the Dockers' Union, who until then had declined to strike because they were outnumbered by non-unionists and were vulnerable to blacklegging, left work and were joined by workers from all sections of the port. The strikers also armed themselves, and soon many of them carried "sticks and bludgeons; clubs with knife-blades and cut-throat razor blades set in the end, rope coshes with nails sticking out from the knots and plenty of weapons"[2]. When the court decided to remand Tupper in custody, dockers and seamen stormed the City Hall, but were beaten back by large numbers of mounted and foot police. They retreated to the docks, stole barrels of stout and bottles of whisky from ships and warehouses, set fire to the Dublin and Liverpool warehouse, attacked the Glasgow warehouse, and pushed a lorry into the dock. Further damage was prevented only by a fierce baton charge by the Cardiff constabulary. During this riot Tupper was in the cells at the City Hall. He had opposed the use of violence but had been unable to prevent it. As most of the men were not members of a union, they were undisciplined and were incapable of conducting a dispute peacefully and effectively. Tupper, however, was released the next day on bail; according to him, the magistrates realised that he was the only person who could prevent more disorder.

Tupper used this opportunity to spread the dispute to ports throughout the Bristol Channel. On 20th July he arrived at the Alexandra dock at Newport with Havelock Wilson and told the dock workers there, "We have got the Shipping Federation whacked and we must get the shipowners down on their knees"[3]. In addition, Tupper stressed the need to prevent the employment of Chinese crews upon British ships, and warned the men that Chinese dock labourers would soon be engaged if this practice was not stopped. In a dramatic gesture he removed his morning coat, raised his arms high above his head and cried out, "What are you going to do tonight? Then I say in God's name and in the name of justice 'down tools' tomorrow morning".[4] Without bothering to consult their own district officials, the men dropped their shovels and left work.

The strikes in Cardiff and Newport did not remain confined to the waterfront. At Cardiff strikers marched to a brewery and bombarded girl workers with potatoes until they finally agreed to strike. They also entered a sweet factory, and dragged out some of the workers during their lunch-time and ate their food. Dray-men, platers, riverters, cigar-makers, and the Cardiff

58

Jewish Amalgamated Society of Tailors, on the other hand, struck voluntarily in sympathy. They were not influenced by the doctrine of syndicalism, but merely supported the port workers' claim and used the opportunity to emphasise their own grievances and wage demands. The strike was also exploited by those who were opposed to the existence of Chinese labourers in Cardiff, and the rumour was spread that Chinese strike-breakers were to be brought to the port by the employers. Racial tension grew, and violent attacks were made upon Chinese lodging houses and laundries by large groups of workers. Premises were stoned and ransacked, and, when mounted police attempted to establish control, the rioters retaliated by throwing bags of starch at the horses, almost blinding them.

The leader of the strike, Captain Tupper, did not advise such disorder, nor did he refer to Mann's philosophy in his speeches. Although he boasted that F. E. Smith once denounced him as "The most dangerous man in Europe" and one whose "ambition was to drench his country in blood from John O'Groats to Land's End",[5] Tupper condemned the use of violence. For instance, when his followers began to cut telegraph wires and to attack the Chinese, he argued,

> You don't want to get smashing Chinese houses, boys. We have got the employers on their knees. You can get all you want without going on in that manner. Don't get excited and break the law, and above all, do not be guilty of any action that would warrant the soldiers coming out... If they wanted to rid themselves of the Chinese the best method was to starve them out.[6]

Moreover, syndicalist influence was reduced by the absence from the region of Alf Cox who had played such a prominent part in the Houlder dispute of 1910. He had been sent by Tom Mann to organise port workers in Liverpool and Belfast, and missed the dock strikes in South Wales.

Even though coal trimmers and tippers at Cardiff, Barry and Port Talbot also responded to Tupper's call to strike, the South Wales port workers were not a united force. Significantly the Swansea dock workers refused to strike. They expressed their willingness not to unload goods from ships which had been black-listed, but were opposed to a general stoppage on the waterfront. Although they had left work on 23rd June in support of the seamen, the Swansea men had later obtained wage increases and felt that their position might be undermined if they supported workers in nearby ports. It was not long, too, before differences between the strikers at Cardiff and Newport became apparent. The Newport dock labourers had a strong tradition of good organisation and were prepared to hold out until their grievances were removed; but at Cardiff the union's roots were weaker, the employers were more hostile to it, and the men's representatives were more inclined to compromise. Consequently solidarity amongst the strikers crumbled, and the labourers of each port put their own interests first.

During the early days of the strike Captain Tupper was in sole command of the men. He organised demonstrations, called out workers in local industries, collected funds and regarded himself as "the uncrowned king of the Bristol Channel."[7] The strikers at each port were also united and backed his proposal that no man would return to work until all demands were accepted. Subsequently, though, strike committees were set up by officials of the Dockers' Union and other organisations who wished to regain control over their members. At Newport the Newport Joint Strike Committee was formed by local men such as J. K. Price, Albert Kenny and John O'Leary of the N.A.L.U., George Jackson of the Seamen, Henry Seer, J. O'Shea and C. Evans of the Dockers, and representatives of the Plumbers, Smiths Hammermen, Boilermakers and the Amalgamated Society of Railway Servants. At Cardiff a strike committee was also established; however, prominent union leaders such as Ernest Bevin of the Bristol Dockers, John Chappell of the Coal Trimmers, John Twomey of the N.A.L.U. and J. H. Thomas of the Railwaymen were members, because apart from the Cardiff Coal Trimmers' Association unionism was weak on the waterfront there. These committees played a major role during the strike. Tillett visited the area on 23rd July, but he soon returned to London where negotiations with the Port of London Authority were in progress.

Due to the large numbers of dock workers and seamen on strike in South Wales, the Shipping Federation was unable to find enough "free" labourers to replace them, and it failed to persuade local authorities to protect its imported blacklegs. Some strike-breakers were brought to Cardiff by the depot ship, *Lady Jocelyn,* but, according to Tupper, they soon deserted when their food was doctored by a friend employed as a cook aboard the ship. The Federation was so impotent that George Jackson claimed, "The Shipping Federation had been 'knackered' and it only wanted a simple knock-out blow to finish it".[8] Yet it was not so easy for the Cardiff strike committee to persuade the Cardiff Railway Company and firms in the city to capitulate. Like the Newport committee it had demanded the closed shop and wage increases, but Cardiff concerns refused to negotiate until the men had returned to their employment. Although work was still at a complete standstill at the port, the Cardiff committee accepted these terms and encouraged the men to resume their jobs. Only Ernest Bevin opposed this settlement, but in the circumstances he was powerless. Unions with more moderate views such as the Coal Trimmers' Association and the Amalgamated Society of Railway Servants, to which the tippers were now affiliated, were reluctant to test the employers' strength and their support was essential. These organisations were also persuaded to compromise by the settlement of the seamen's dispute on 26th July.

The development of waterfront unionism in Cardiff was therefore considerably influenced by the attitude of the Cardiff Railway Company. The company firmly rejected the men's demands, and it was supported by smaller firms on the Cardiff waterfront. In spite of the unions being stronger than at any time since 1890, their officials compromised because they were afraid to risk defeat. Dockers' and N.A.L.U. leaders at Newport, on the other hand, were unwilling to act similarly. They were opposed by a concern which had never been hostile to unionism, and had the full support of the men. The Newport port workers remained on strike and continued to press the same proposals. One of their leaders, J. K. Price, wrote,

> Cardiff had many times fattened at the expense of Newport. I stated that Newport was out for a Bristol Channel arrangement, and if the Cardiff people chose to sell their neighbours at any rate Newport would fight on and win single handed. It is pleasing to know that Newport had been true to tradition.[9]

The resolute action of the Newport port workers persuaded their employers to capitulate, and on 31st July an agreement was signed. The Newport Joint Strike Committee and the Newport Employers' Committee decided that the unions involved in the dispute would gain preference of employment for their members, that the grievances of the men would be alleviated, and that work would begin again immediately on the waterfront. All sections of the labour force benefited substantially from this settlement: hydraulic cranemen gained 1/- per week, casual deal carriers obtained 8d. per day, and the coal tippers achieved an increase of 3/- per 100 tons to be shared between four men. The Newport Strike Committee was very pleased with these gains, for it stressed that,

> The Newport employer is almost without exception a man to be proud of, he takes no mean advantage of the workman's weakness in conference, and is less snobbish to the workman than the workman is to his mate, and as far as the more experienced Newport employer is concerned he does not grumble about the high wages earned, he is fully aware of the human sacrifice involved in the dispatch given to the shipping of Newport by the workmen ere those wages reach his pockets and he has no desire to drag his men down to the level of the casual docker in many of our large seaport towns.[10]

The strike, furthermore, led to an increase in the strength of the union at Newport: membership contributions from waterfront workers in the first six months of 1911 totalled £282, but between July and December they amounted to £484. At Cardiff, Barry and Swansea contributions also rose during the same period from £132 to £910, from £97 to £169, and from £838 to £895 respectively.

The victory of the Newport dock workers influenced some of the smaller concerns in Cardiff, and union officials were able to negotiate concessions, even though the Cardiff labourers had returned to work. Nevertheless, the Cardiff Railway Company was still not prepared to reach a settlement, nor would it accept the port rates agreed between the union and merchants. The considerable difference between the level of wages of the company's employees and the port workers at Newport and Swansea thus remained.

Wage-rates at Newport, Swansea and Cardiff docks in August 1911[11]

	Newport	Swansea	Cardiff
Constant cranemen	36/- per week	35/- per week	25/- per week
Casual cranemen	7/- per day	(No casual) cranemen at this port)	5/- per day
General cargo-men: hold work	Piece-work: average 8/- per day	Piece-work: average 8/- per day	Day-work: 6/- per day
Pit props: hold work	Piece-work: average 8/- per day	Piece work: average 8/- per day	Day-work: 6/- per day
Pit props: shore work	Piece-work: average 8/- per day	Piece-work: average 8/- per day	Day-work: 5/- per day

Table 5

The attitude of the company and the unbelligerence of union officials persuaded the pitprop carriers, general cargo workers, iron-ore labourers and cranemen to declare another unofficial strike at Cardiff docks on 15th August. Yet the Cardiff Railway Company continued to refuse to raise wages and to recognise the Dockers' Union. Colonel Denniss, its General Manager, declined to meet Bevin and local union officials, though he offered to negotiate with the company's own workmen. The deadlock was broken only by the intervention of the Board of Trade. An agreement was formulated, and the strikers returned to work two weeks later. The firm still refused to recognise the union, but it undertook to examine the men's grievances and agreed to submit the matter to arbitration if necessary. The company's wage proposals were in fact later rejected by the general cargomen, and arbitration proceedings began at the City Hall in Cardiff in February 1912. The umpire of this court, Mr. A. A. Hudson K.C., eventually decided that the wages of most groups should be advanced: constant crane drivers were awarded 2/- per week increase, casual crane drivers gained an extra 1/- per day, but general cargo workers received no improvement in their rates of pay. In spite of this award, the level of wages of the Cardiff port labourers remained inferior in comparison with the earnings of men at Newport and Swansea. The day-work system of payment also persisted at Cardiff, and dockers were employed on a more casual basis. Even though the membership of the Dockers' Union had increased considerably there because of these strikes (see Appendix Two), the strength and attitude of the Cardiff Railway Company continued to retard its progress.

The Newport dock workers, however, were able to take full advantage of the favourable economic conditions of the time. Although they did not break their agreement with local employers, the men proposed that the terms of the settlement should also apply to Houlder Brothers who were still insisting that the day-work system should prevail at Newport so far as their own ships were concerned. In September 1911 the Newport Strike Committee decided that all transport work at the port would be halted immediately unless Houlders accepted the piece-work method of payment, and persuaded Swansea dock workers to assist it. In October the Swansea men refused to load a Houlder Brothers' vessel, the *Hornby Grange,* and to discharge another, the *Valhalla* in early December. The Industrial Council of the Board of Trade tried to settle the dispute, but Houlders would not compromise and insisted that Sir David Harrel's arbitration agreement of 1910 should be adhered to. Houlders, though, did take notice of the National Transport Workers' Federation's decision in December to "black" their vessels in every port in the United Kingdom and abroad until the issue was settled. Less than two weeks later negotiations began between representatives of the shipping firm and the Newport Strike Committee, and an agreement was signed. Harrel's award was modified: although the day-work system was retained, it was decided that the general cargo workers were to be given a wage increase and that the master stevedores were to be allowed a free hand in the choice of men to be hired.

Houlders, the Newport Strike Committee and the National Transport Workers' Federation were satisfied with this settlement; yet the Newport general cargo workers were not, because Houlders' blacklegs were eligible for employment under the new terms. The dockers were bitterly opposed to Houlders' insistence that their labourers should join the Dockers' Union in order to enhance their chance of obtaining work:

> When we understood that we were expected to work alongside men who had come in to take our jobs while we were fighting for the custom of the port we, of course, kicked against it . . . If all the negotiations and struggles amount to this, then I say that the Strike Committee did not know their business and certainly should not have signed the agreement, which is going to benefit the men against whom they have been fighting.[12]

The men therefore declined to admit Houlders' employees into their organisation, refused to handle any of the company's goods, and turned for help once again to Alf Cox who had recently returned from Belfast.

The action of the general cargo workers was strongly repudiated by the

Executive Committee of the National Transport Workers' Federation which refused to give them any more assistance in their struggle. But the Executive Committee's decision played into the hands of Cox who was able to utilise the men's anger over the Houlder dispute and the closed shop issue for his own ends. He called an emergency meeting at the Dockers' Institute in January 1912 and representatives of every section of the Dockers' Union at the port attended. Opposition to the moderate views of local union leaders such as Seer and O'Shea was obviously strong, because it was decided to set up an Emergency and Advisory Committee to deal with all future disputes. Alf Cox was elected Chairman and Percy Knight, a seaman with syndicalist views, was appointed Secretary. The power to declare a strike at the port was thus transferred from the Dockers' officials to the syndicalists. Nevertheless, the strength of the new committee proved to be illusory. As we shall see later, Cox was unable to persuade the rank and file to strike over issues which were unlikely to benefit them financially.

The 1912 strike and its consequences

During 1911 the National Transport Workers' Federation had much influence in London where it represented the main waterside unions and successfully negotiated wage increases following a general stoppage in August. In the provinces, on the other hand, the N.T.W.F. had less control. Although a committee of the N.T.W.F. was formed in the Bristol Channel district in March 1912, it was weakened by the decision of the Cardiff Coal Trimmers' Association not to join. Furthermore, few of the rank and file at Newport were sympathetic towards the Federation's Executive Committee which had refused to give any more help to the general cargo workers of the port against Houlder Brothers. There was greater support for the Federation at Swansea and Bristol; when the N.T.W.F. called on its members in the provinces to join a national strike in June 1912, dockers at these two ports left work. However, trade unionists in other towns refused to assist them, and the strike swiftly collapsed.

The decision of the N.T.W.F. to declare a national stoppage was closely linked to events at the port of London. On 19th May, 1912 members of the Lightermen's Society began militant action in London and on the Medway, and four days later the dispute was turned into a general strike at the port by the N.T.W.F.'s Executive. It gave assistance because the Lightermen's difficulties were concerned with the closed shop, and it was felt that a showdown with the employers over this question would have occurred anyway sooner or later. Most workers on the waterfront also had grievances and generally favoured another confrontation while trade was still increasing. Though these issues were peculiar only to London, it was decided to appeal to port workers throughout Britain to back the London men by striking on 10th June. It was considered that such action would prevent the employers from diverting ships from London to trouble-free areas and from obtaining an adequate supply of blackleg labour.

Despite Tillett's confidence that the provinces would agree with this decision, the N.T.W.F. failed to obtain much support. At Cardiff, Dockers' members believed that if they broke their agreement with the employers they would never be able to make another satisfactory settlement, and that it was useless to become involved without the help of the coal trimmers and tippers who had decided not to strike. Similarly, workmen at Barry, Port Talbot and Newport declined to leave work because the Cardiff labourers refused to do so, and because their union did not provide financial aid. At Newport the men were also influenced by the Houlder dispute. According to J. K. Price of the National Amalgamated Labourers' Union,

> The dock labourers of the port will not hurriedly strike..They are sick and tired of strikes. Their own domestic difficulties have been sufficiently harrassing during the past two years and support from other quarters, especially London, has been meagre indeed. The non-unionists, created over the Houlder dispute, partially through the laxity

of effort on the part of the transport workers are still with us; in fact they have been sent to London to break up the strike there, and whatever happens it is practically certain that after all this stir is over the same canker worm will exist.[13]

Although Alf Cox, the leader of the general cargo workers, favoured a stoppage, militancy was not approved by his fellow workmen who decided to refuse only to unload ships diverted from London. The sole assistance that Cox managed to give to the strikers was some money which he collected by playing a barrel-organ in the streets of Newport's dockland.

Nonetheless, at the port of Swansea the dockers walked out, and were fully supported by the patent fuel workers at the Graigola Fuel Works, the Atlantic Works and the Pacific Works. On 11th June a meeting was held on the waterfront, and the men resolved not to resume work until they we. ordered back by their officials. At Swansea there was greater sympathy for the N.T.W.F. because two local men were on its Executive Committee: Robert Williams, a former coal trimmer and Councillor at Swansea, was General Secretary, and John Twomey, the General Secretary of the N.A.L.U., was a committee member. Many of the men, too, felt that if they did not help the London port workers the Shipping Federation would become powerful again. Yet it also appears that the Swansea dock workers decided to "down tools" partly because of a mistake made by their officials. At their meeting the men were informed that the Port Talbot and Newport dockers had already left work, and before it was discovered that an error had occurred they themselves struck.

Bristol port workers also backed the N.T.W.F. by joining the action, but they were considerably weakened by the lack of enthusiasm for the strike in South Wales and other parts of the country. Although one of their officials, Ernest Bevin, travelled to Cardiff and Newport, he was unable to persuade the local port workers to extend the dispute. As a result it was ended in Bristol two days later by the Bristol strike committee which decided that it would be in the men's interests to resume employment before the stoppage was broken by waterfront concerns. On 17th June, Swansea dockers and patent fuel workmen also voted to 'throw in the towel'.

Lacking support in provincial ports, the strike committee in London was eventually forced to capitulate and ordered a return to work on 29th July. Its attempt at organising the first national dock strike had failed for two main reasons. In the first place, labourers at the waterside had had little sense of national solidarity, and were more concerned with preserving their own local agreements. In addition, the strike leaders had shown little foresight, for they had believed that the port workers could succeed by national action as the miners had done in a national strike in April 1912. But they forgot that trimmers and tippers in South Wales and the North of England had suffered considerably from the miners' stoppage, and would want instead to make up their lost wages.

66

In London the collapse of the strike led to a decline in the membership of the Dockers' Union on the waterfront. The employers also weakened its attempt to gain preference of employment for members by subsequently hiring all workmen inside the dock gates. The men who had been involved in the dispute at Bristol and Swansea, on the other hand, were treated more leniently by their firms, and the Dockers' Union remained strong in the Bristol Channel region. Only in Port Talbot did the membership of Tillett's organisation seriously decline. In this port most of the coal trimmers left to form their own union, the Port Talbot Dockers' Association, because they disagreed with the policies of the Dockers' district secretary at Port Talbot, Jonah Charles. The coal trimmers several years previously had formed regular gangs and had completely excluded other workers from employment, even members of the Dockers' Union; but Charles had demanded that the work should be shared, and had eventually forced the trimmers to comply. The new system was not popular with the regular coal trimmers, nor was Charles' readiness to cause disputes and his support for syndicalism. They were the elite of the labour force and had gained increases without the use of strike action, and complained that,

> Since Mr. Jonah Charles came to the dock five years ago it had been made into a den of strikes and wrangling, and personal and family disputes. For ten years previous to Mr. Charles' advent the men settled their own affairs and there had not been one hour's stoppage. Mr. Charles had upset that condition of things by autocratic tyranny and total disregard of the men.[14]

Thus, when the national transport strike broke out, they used it as an excuse to leave the Dockers' Union and to revert to the old method of hiring.

As the Port Talbot coal trimmers had strong bargaining power and opposed the use of militant action, the Port Talbot Dockers' Association gained recognition from the local employers. The new society was also able to enforce the closed shop, and persuaded the dock company to sack thirty two members of the Dockers' Union who had responded to the N.T.W.F.'s call for a national strike. Since this setback followed soon after the collapse of the strike in the Bristol Channel, the Dockers' Union was unwilling to retaliate. In spite of a stoppage by 250 dock and wharf labourers at Port Talbot against the company's decision in July 1912, the men were not assisted by Tillett's organisation and were forced to return to work a week later.

The influence of the trimmers' society remained unchecked, and it continued to demand the monopoly of work for its members. In April 1913 it again persuaded the Port Talbot Dock Company to dismiss a number of dockers who belonged to the Dockers' Union, but on this occasion the men's officials felt that they were able to challenge the employers. At each of the Bristol Channel ports the union's membership was substantial, because concerns had not been sufficiently provoked by the 1912 dispute to counter-attack, and trade remained at a high level. Bevin and Orbell were therefore sent to Port Talbot to request the dockers' reinstatement, and they were supported by Tupper who called a strike of seamen at Port Talbot and persuaded Vernon Hartshorn, the Miners' leader, to stop coal being sent to the docks. His action forced the company to reinstate the men several days later and to agree to submit the question of whether or not the coal trimmers should rejoin the Dockers' organisation to arbitration. The arbitration award subsequently favoured the Dockers' Union, for it led to the dock company and a prominent coal firm, North's Navigation Company, discontinuing their recognition of the Coal Trimmers' Association and denying its members preference of employment. By April 1914 the Association was dissolved, and its members were enrolled again by the Dockers' Union.

Tillett's union, however, still remained unable to undermine the Cardiff Coal Trimmers' Association which continued to enforce the closed shop and to be recognised by employers at Cardiff. Robert Williams and Harry Gosling, the President of the N.T.W.F., also failed in April 1913 to persuade the Trimmers' Association to join the Transport Workers' Federation, because its members doubted the advantage of belonging to an organisation which largely consisted of labourers less skilled than themselves. Nevertheless, the C.C.T.A. later found that the support of other unions was useful to promote its own demands. In July 1913 it attended a national conference of coal trimmers and tippers at Birmingham along with representatives of the Dockers' Union, the N.A.L.U., the National Union of Dock Labourers, the Tyneside Teemers' and Trimmers' Union and other associations, and considered ways to bring about a cessation of work in the coal export industry between 1 p.m. on Saturday and 6 a.m. on the following Monday for each successive week. It was decided to give the dock companies notice that this change would come into effect in September 1913. The Hull and Tyne trimmers eventually compromised with their employers, but the coal trimmers at each of the Bristol Channel ports enforced the decision of the conference and maintained the ban on overtime until the outbreak of the First World War. The success of this policy persuaded the Cardiff Coal Trimmers' Association that the benefits of united action were profound, and it joined the N.T.W.F. in June 1914.

By the early months of 1914 the position of the Dockers' Union in the Bristol Channel ports had thus been strengthened. The Port Talbot coal trimmers had rejoined, and it had formed a closer relationship with the Cardiff Coal Trimmers' Association. Many of its waterfront branches also retained a large number of their members, and enforced the closed shop at various hiring centres. In addition, because trade conditions remained favourable, the union was able to negotiate wage increases. Substantial advances were even achieved at Cardiff by casual grain workers, timber porters and deal runners who were employed by stevedores and merchants. Although the Cardiff Railway Company still refused to recognise the union and to improve the wages of its rank and file, it seemed at last that the

Dockers' organisation had established itself on the Cardiff waterfront. For the first time its officials had sufficient opportunity to strengthen the union's roots at the port, and they persuaded some of the smaller concerns to give their members preference of employment. As a result the workers became more loyal, and a greater sense of discipline was developed amongst them.

The collapse of the national strike in June 1912 had little lasting effect upon the port workers of South Wales. Though many matters were settled by conciliation between 1912 and 1914, dockers still showed their willingness to strike unofficially whenever it suited them. Yet these disputes were of short duration and chiefly involved local issues. The most serious stoppage took place on the Swansea waterfront between August 15th and 19th, 1913, when 3000 men left work following the arrest of a dock labourer, William Lewis, at the Tennant Wharf. While Lewis had been unloading pitprops a member of the Swansea Harbour police force, P. C. Llewellyn, had heard him swear. Llewellyn objected to the labourer's obscene language, and a fight occurred which led to Lewis' arrest. Because of this incident the union's membership at the docks came out on strike, and strongly demanded Lewis' release and Llewellyn's dismissal from the service. But the presence of several delegates of the Dockers' Union upon the Swansea Harbour Trust helped to quickly settle the issue. A meeting between these officials and the employers' representatives on the Trust was held three days later, and it was decided that a full enquiry into the whole matter would take place after the case was heard in court. Consequently the dockers decided to return to work, but they threatened to strike again if the result of this enquiry was not satisfactory. In the meanwhile, though, the employers' representatives arranged that no evidence be given against Lewis, and when he eventually appeared in court, his case was dismissed. Good industrial relations were thus restored at the port because of the close contact between union leaders and employing concerns.

Although no prolonged strike was fought at the Bristol Channel ports after July 1912, evidence suggests that a major confrontation between the Seamen's and Dockers' Unions and the shipowners might have developed but for the outbreak of the First World War. After 1912 an increasing number of Chinese labourers were hired on board British ships, particularly at Barry Dock, at lower rates than British sailors. This practice was opposed by the Sailors' and Firemen's Union which began in March 1914 to hold up ships in various ports. In the same month delegates from the Bristol Channel section of the N.T.W.F. also decided to arrange mass meetings at all of the major seaports in the United Kingdom to see whether workers in these areas would protest against the employment of Chinese labour. They agreed to warn dock companies of the dangers of a possible stoppage of work over this issue and to send a deputation to persuade John Burns, the President of the Board of Trade, to enforce the language test for Asiatic sailors. However, the outbreak of war shortly after prevented vessels with Chinese crews being held up on a national basis. Whether such action would have been attempted if the war had not occurred is obviously questionable, but it is possible that, because of the strength of the Dockers' and Seamen's organisations in South Wales and because this area had become the "cockpit" of the Chinese labour issue, shipping might seriously have been disrupted there.

Even though the collapse of the strike in 1912 did not significantly affect the South Wales port workers, members of the N.T.W.F.'s Executive Committee were influenced considerably, and began to seriously think in terms of transforming their federation into an amalgamation which would be more effective. They set up a committee, and the matter was discussed at the N.T.W.F.'s conference at Newport in 1913. On 8th July, 1914 an important gathering of unions was also convened at the Caxton Hall, Westminster, to discuss the Executive's proposals. At this meeting a vote was taken, and twenty six unions were in favour, two against and two were undecided. It is significant that one of the two societies which did not arrive at a decision was the Cardiff Coal Trimmers' Association. Despite its affiliation to the N.T.W.F., the Coal Trimmers' Association was not prepared to sacrifice the privileged employment position of its members. If it had amalgamated with these unions, work would have been shared with labourers on the Cardiff waterfront as it was at Port Talbot. Yet, before the Coal Trimmers' officials made a final decision, war broke out and amalgamation was postponed until 1921.

The growth of the Dockers' Union in the tinplate and other industries, 1911-14.

Despite the occurrence of industrial conflict on the waterfront, the tinplate industry was not seriously disrupted between 1911-14, and matters continued to be settled by the Conciliation Board. Wage increases were requested by workers, but the Dockers' leaders remained reluctant to force their members' claims. In June 1911, although the men's call for a general wage advance of 10% was rejected by the employers, Tillett and his executive refused to use strike action. Instead, the Dockers' officials accepted the tinplate companies' argument that wage increases were unjustified because the demand for tinplates was slowly declining, and promised not to press demands until trade again improved significantly and unless four months' notice was given. Their attitude certainly helped to keep the industry free from stoppages, but it did not assist their members very much.

The Dockers' policy was much criticised by its tinplate branches, especially in Morriston, and the *Dockers' Record* remarked that several centres "have been the cause of considerable trouble to the officers on account of the little appreciation shown to the union, its officers and the benefits the men are receiving."[15] Tillett was so concerned that Seer of Newport, Lock of Cardiff, Abel Evans of Gloucester, Orbell, Wignall and himself spent some time in the tinplate district in an attempt to reconcile their members. The men remained in the Dockers' Union, but their decision was not influenced by Tillett's activities alone. Undoubtedly they appreciated the fact that, even though their union had done little to press their claims, none of the other organisations had been any more militant. The Steel Smelters' Union, for instance, fined members who struck unofficially.

Dockers' leaders remained reluctant to turn the issue of increased wages into a major conflict, for their union was involved in large disputes at the ports from July onwards and the regular contributions of the tinplate workers were needed. Although they again submitted a claim for a general advance of 10% at a meeting of the Conciliation Board in 1912, their proposals were not strongly emphasised and were modified by the employers. The Dockers' representatives were so conciliatory that Wignall was thanked by F. W. Gibbins, the President of the Welsh Plate and Sheet Manufacturers' Association, for "the way the business had been got through with no waste of words and 'no playing to the gallery' but with a desire to conduct important business in a business-like manner."[16] Yet, despite their officials' attitude, the tinplate workers did not act unofficially and try to remove their grievances themselves, because they realised that the firms were well organised.

The Dockers' Union, on the other hand, did help to improve the conditions of employment in the tinplate industry. In 1912 the working week was shortened when the Conciliation Board agreed that all mills in the industry should be on eight-hour shifts; and by 1914 all works closed at noon on Saturday, whereas in 1900 they had not closed until 4 p.m. on Saturday. By

1912 a change had also been made in the period of payment of wages, and workers were paid every fortnight instead of monthly. Little was done, though, to improve working conditions in the mills and tinhouses. According to two factory inspectors, E.L. Collis and J. Hilditch, in 1912 tinhouse workers ran much risk of accident from the splashing of molten metals, fumes and dust, and the unguarded machinery. Yet, as W. Minchinton points out, exacting conditions also existed in other industries, and thus the deficiencies of the tinplate industry did not arouse the conscience of the time.

In order to minimise its involvement in trade disputes the Dockers' Union continued to try to establish conciliation boards in South Wales. In 1911 it finally persuaded the copper employers to set up a Copper Trade Conciliation Board with a similar constitution to the Tinplate Board. Discussion chiefly centred around the issues of wages and working conditions, and militant action was largely prevented. However, stoppages occurred in industries where the union had been unable to establish such a board. A dispute, for instance, was fought at the dry docks in Cardiff, Newport, Barry and Penarth during August and September 1911 involving the Dockers' Union and N.A.L.U. Both organisations had recruited lower-paid workmen such as platers' helpers and fitters' labourers at the dry docks, and were implicated because the employers alleged that an agreement made in January 1911 had been broken. The agreement which had given the men an extra 2/- a week and had set up a code of rules concerning working conditions had not been acceptable to the N.A.L.U.'s members who had persuaded their officials to adopt a different set of rules. Their action led the companies to lock out all workers for a month before a settlement was made. It was finally decided to increase wages by 6d. per day, but not to make any further alterations in the existing agreement.

During this period a large number of workers in other industries also joined the Dockers' Union, as they were influenced by the port workers' victories which had been well publicised. Having firmly established itself on the waterfront, Tillett's union, too, paid greater attention to their recruitment than it had done previously. In order to increase their funds and to organise potential blackleggers, its officials spent a considerable amount of time enrolling labourers throughout South Wales. Between 1911 and 1914 brewery workers and carters at Newport, rope workers, copper workers and mineral-water salesmen at Cardiff, grave-diggers at Barry, tube workers at Pontnewydd, tram workers and carters at Swansea, engineering workers at Morriston, and chemical workers and galvanizers at Llanelly were recruited.

In some of these industries disputes later occurred which brought about increases for the workmen concerned. Nonetheless, they did not arouse as much interest as the strikes at the South Wales ports had done, because events on the waterside had been more dramatic. Due to the casual system of employment at the docks and wharves, the men there were more vulnerable to blacklegging. Consequently they had sought support from workers in local industries in order to strengthen their position, and had acted more militantly. The over-supply of labour thus continued to influence significantly industrial relations at the ports.

NOTES

1. *Cambria Daily Leader*, June 30, 1911.
2. Edward Tupper, *Seamen's Torch*, London, 1938, p.44.
3. *South Wales Argus*, July 20, 1911.
4. Ibid.
5. Tupper, op.cit., pp.14, 72.
6. *Cambria Daily Leader*, July 22, 1911.
7. Tupper, op.cit., p.31.
8. *South Wales Daily News*, July 21, 1911.
9. J.K. Price, *The Newport Dock Strike of 1911*, Newport, 1911, p.7.
10. Ibid., pp. 23-4.
11. *South Wales Argus*, August 25, 1911.
12. *South Wales Daily News*, December 30, 1911.
13. *South Wales Argus*, June 11, 1912.
14. *Cambria Daily Leader*, June 24, 1912.
15. *Dockers' Record*, June, 1911, p.2.
16. *South Wales Daily News*, June 19, 1912.

9. Two opponents of the
   Dockers' Union:
   a. Sir William Thomas Lewis

and b. Mr. Frank Houlder

10. J. Havelock Wilson, leader of the Seamen's Union, leaving the Law
    Courts, Cardiff, in July 1911 following the release of Captain Edward
    Tupper

11. Tupper on a balcony in Bute Street, Cardiff, addresses dockers and seamen during the 1911 dock strike

12. Blacklegs at work. Edward England's clerks unloading potatoes during the 1911 dock strike at Cardiff

13. Out in sympathy! Cardiff coal trimmers leave their work at the docks and march through the city in support of the dockers' pay claim of 1911

14. Mass support for the National Amalgamated Labourers' Union at Swansea, as several hundred dockers march through the town in 1911

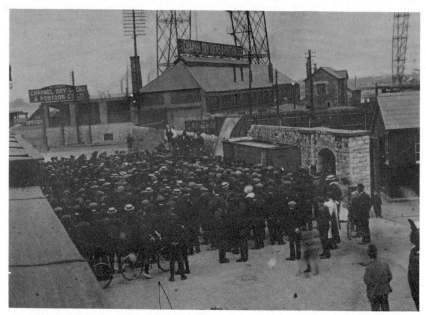

15. In the shadows of Newport Transporter Bridge, which spans the River Usk, Captain Edward Tupper addresses a group of Newport dockers outside the dock gates

16. The Newport Strike Committee of 1911. *Back Row,* from left of picture: T.A. Sundy, M. Lynch, A.J. Kenny, J.K. Price. *Front Row,* H. Seer, G. Jackson, J. O'Leary, J. McAuley

Chapter 4
War and its Aftermath

The development of the Dockers' Union at the ports during the First World War

The outbreak of the First World War presented the Dockers' Union with a number of problems. The recruitment into the Army of 1,500 members at Cardiff, over 1,000 at Swansea and many others at Newport, Port Talbot and Barry meant that the union lost contributions. In addition, those remaining on the waterfront were badly affected by the decline of trade especially during the early months of the war. Although some dockers were hired by the Government to dig trenches and by local councils to build houses, unemployment still persisted. At the same time the cost of living rose sharply, and union officials had difficulty in preventing members with strong bargaining power from striking. The Dockers' leaders opposed strikes in order to help the war effort, and because they feared that the closed shop at several ports might be undermined by the Shipping Federation and the Government if the rank and file continued to act recklessly. How effective they were in preventing militant action and overcoming their organisation's other difficulties must now be examined.

Although many important strikes had been fought since 1910, trade union leaders declared an industrial truce in August 1914. Nevertheless, because of rising prices, some workers were reluctant to accept their officials' policy. On the waterfront the coal trimmers vigorously pressed their demands, and were especially militant at Newport. In October trimmers loading three steamers struck for increased wages and refused conciliation. The employers, Tatem and Radcliffe, were forced to appeal to the Shipping Federation, and blacklegs were sent from London to complete the stowing. Fortunately for the union, the Newport trimmers agreed not to repeat this action and to submit all future disputes to their conciliation board. The trimmers were wise to support conciliation, for many workers were unemployed at the time and could have been hired by waterside concerns to strike-break. In industries such as engineering and shipbuilding stoppages were more serious, and consequently the Government decided to seek greater powers over labour in industry. In March 1915 Government ministers and trade union leaders met at the Treasury, and agreed that until the end of the war issues would be settled by conciliation or compulsory arbitration. To help the war effort it was also decided to relax trade practices, and to allow longer hours and the employment of unskilled and women workers. Four months later the Government passed the Munitions of War Act which gave it statutory powers in matters covered by this agreement. The Act applied to the munitions industry, but was soon extended to cover all essential industries. Strikes became illegal, and grievances had to be referred to compulsory arbitration. Trade practices were also suspended and the profits of munition firms were limited.

The *Dockers' Record* was very critical of the Munitions Act:

Under the terms of the Munitions of War Act, 1915, the right to strike was, amongst other things, patriotically abrogated in exchange for the right to arbitration. What we now appear to possess is neither, for the arbitrators are directed to refuse advances except under certain conditions where such adjustments are proved to be necessary. Is this arbitration? Is this fair dealing? Emphatically no. There is but one fitting term for it and that is sharp practice.[1]

Yet Tillett and his officials did not advise their members to break the law. Although the union did not suspend dispute pay, its leaders continued to try to prevent strikes. Their task was made easier because most workers didn't wish to be fined for contravening the Act, and disputes did not involve any of the major issues which had caused great conflict on the waterfront before 1914. No problems occurred at Newport over the loading of Houlders' ships, because the general cargo workers agreed to do this work during the war; i 'r at Cardiff over the question of union recognition, for the Cardiff Railway Company finally recognised the Dockers' Union in 1915 as a result of the war and the introduction of compulsory arbitration. Some unofficial stoppages did take place during this period at Cardiff, Newport, Penarth and Port Talbot concerning the rates and the working conditions for unloading iron pyrites, but they were not serious and were quickly settled by arbitration. They appeared to be important only because it was war-time; before 1914 small disputes such as these had occurred regularly and with much less publicity.

The coal trimmers, on the other hand, became increasingly militant particularly at Newport. Although the Newport trimmers had agreed in 1914 to allow all disputes to be settled by their conciliation board, they frequently stopped work in 1916. Their bargaining power had been strengthened by the growing shortage of labour and the congestion of traffic at the port, and they were able to press their demands strongly. Even though they were given a 12½% war bonus in 1915, they refused to unload neutral ships except for double the normal tariff and demanded substantial payments for British and Allied tonnage. The *Dockers' Record* warned that, "Power of organisation should be used where necessary, but not abused"[2], but union officials could not control them as the men wished to fully exploit their position. When their request for further increases was turned down by the employers, they called a conference of trimmers from the Bristol Channel ports and agreed to stop all negotiations and to force their demands. Their decision was opposed by the dock companies and coal shippers who complained to the Government. As a result of a Government enquiry a meeting of firms and workmen was held, and it was decided to form a Joint Conciliation Board to cover the ports of Newport, Cardiff, Barry, Port Talbot and Swansea. It was also agreed to increase the wage-rates for Bristol Channel coal trimmers, and a 25% war bonus was added to the existing trimming rate.

Until the end of the war the Joint Conciliation Board successfully prevented any more disputes at the ports, but the employers were forced to pay increases to the Bristol Channel coal trimmers to save the coal trade from disruption. In 1917 and 1918 the trimmers received further war bonuses of 22½% and 20%, and obtained many "extras" (that is, supplementary charges for loading particular vessels) and generous overtime rates. Wages thus rose considerably: in 1919 the *South Wales Argus* reported that a number of men at Newport docks were earning between £2,000 and £3,000 a year. According also to Frank Kendall, who was Chairman of the cargo workers' branch at Newport in 1920, by 1918 many coal trimmers at the port earned over £30 a week by piece-work and overtime, and wages of £60 a week were not uncommon. Moreover, their position at the hiring-centres was safeguarded: the Newport trimmers' branch passed a rule that no man would be employed as a regular trimmer unless his father was a coal trimmer and unless he had been registered with the union at birth.

Significant gains were also achieved during this period by other dockers at the ports of South Wales, for the war strengthened the bargaining power of all workers on the waterfront.

Day-rates at Cardiff, Port Talbot and Swansea docks in 1914 and 1919[3].

Port	Day-Rates 1914	Day-Rates 1919
	Day-Rates	**Day-Rates**
Port	**1914**	**1919**
Cardiff	6/6d.	13/9d.
Port Talbot	8/-	15/1½d.
Swansea	7/-	15/6d.

Table 6

Furthermore, the war helped to bring about an important change in the method of conducting wage settlements. Before 1914 all negotiations were conducted locally, but during the war the Government encouraged the unions to negotiate national wage agreements. Bevin approved of this, because he felt that it would lead not only to substantial wage advances but would strengthen the unions by creating a common interest among all workmen in the same industry. He recommended that the National Transport Workers' Federation would represent the men, and it subsequently negotiated some important gains. In January 1918 a national settlement was signed on behalf of the carters; in March 1918 a national advance was given to tram and bus workers; then, in May 1918 a national award was agreed for the general cargo workers. The cargo workers had claimed 8d. per hour advance over pre-war rates, but were given 7d. However, as the *Dockers' Record* stressed, "The result is a triumph for the Federation in general, and our own union in particular"[4]. The success of the Federation advanced the case for amalgamating the various unions when the war ended.

The position of the Dockers' members at the ports was thus advanced considerably during the war. Wages, especially those of coal trimmers, grain workers and iron-ore workers, improved significantly, and hours of work were also reduced at Newport and Swansea after 1917. These settlements were negotiated by the union's leaders and encouraged the men to remain loyal to it. Yet prices also increased rapidly after 1914. According to W. T. Layton and G. Crowther, the cost of living rose by over 100% between July 1914 and July 1918. Nonetheless, port workers definitely did not suffer much from the "timelag" between the rising cost of living and the increases in their own incomes, because the Government and the employers readily approved advances in order to avoid disputes.

The Dockers' Union was also strengthened by the setting up of registration schemes in the ports of South Wales after 1916, for they helped it gain greater control over hiring procedures and over its members. These schemes were principally intended to ensure that each port had an adequate supply of labour while army recruitment was in progress. In 1916 the Board of Trade had decided to place dock work within the bounds of the Military Service Act and to grant certificates of exemption to workmen employed at the ports. In order to select which men should be exempted, Port Labour Committees composed of union representatives, firms and the military authorities were set up at the principal ports. But these committees were unable to perform their work effectively, because they had difficulty in finding out how many dockers were available for work and ensuring that exemptions were given only to regular port workers. As a result they introduced schemes of registration to enhance their efficiency.

Registration involved the control of a pool of labour by a committee representing the employers and workmen of the port. Under such a scheme the employers agreed to hire only men from the pool who carried a badge or ticket issued by the committee. This system was fully approved by the Dockers' leaders, as they realised that registration would enable them to achieve more control over their members and help to restrict the Government from introducing troops at the ports to relieve congestion. Registration had been tried before the war at Liverpool, Goole and Sunderland. At Liverpool, the Liverpool Dock Scheme had been established in 1912 as a step towards decasualisation. All dock labourers had been registered and given a numbered tally, and it had been agreed that only tally holders would be engaged and that the further issue of tallies would be controlled by a committee of company and labour representatives. Although the Liverpool scheme had not been completely successful, it must have influenced the Port Labour Committees in the Bristol Channel area. By August 1916 registration procedures were in force in the main ports, and the union's card was generally accepted to be the token of the Port Labour Committees. Only at Cardiff had an objection been made to the system. The Cardiff Docks Manager did not initially approve, probably because it put the employers and union on an equal footing; but Bevin and Donovan, the local Dockers' secretary, finally managed to persuade him to agree. The registration schemes in the Bristol Channel ports benefited the union considerably, because they prevented outsiders from competing with regular workers at the docks and increased its bargaining power.

Registration, though, did not ensure that dock workers worked regularly and efficiently. The Board of Trade Employment Department, in particular, soon became aware of the schemes' deficiencies, and in the early months of 1917 it tried to introduce a tally system at each of the principal ports. The men's right to employment, it proposed to the Port Labour Committees, would depend not upon union registration cards but on a tally issued by the Board of Trade, and dockers who failed to obtain work at the calling-on stands would have to report to their local Labour Exchange. Its recommendations were vigorously rejected by Dockers' officials, for if workers had had to possess these tallies to gain employment there would have been no need for them to remain in their organisation. Yet the issue did not split the Port Labour Committees, as waterfront concerns respected the union's need to retain the closed shop, and both sides co-operated to find an alternative solution.

At Cardiff it was decided that every transport worker of military age would possess a certificate of exemption issued by the Cardiff Port Labour Committee on behalf of the Board of Trade. Moreover, the men had to hand over their trade union registration cards to their employers who retained them while they were working. At Swansea the Board of Trade's scheme was tried for a short time and workers were registered by the Labour Exchange, but the scheme was dropped after only two weeks because of opposition from the rank and file. Instead, port workers were subsequently registered at the Dockers' offices, and wore union badges which were numbered to correspond with their registration numbers. It was also agreed that unemployed workmen would assemble at a centre where they would be given the option of seeking jobs elsewhere during the remaining part of the day. Finally, at Newport the Port Labour Committee decided in 1917 to give Registration Employment Certificates to each transport worker and to introduce a central hiring-stand to reduce unemployment.

Due to registration Dockers' officials were able to safeguard the position of their members at the hiring-centres and to exert greater control over them, for they could issue registration cards only to dockers not in arrears with union subscriptions. Members were unable to prevent the union from gaining this control, because, whereas port workers at Liverpool had struck against registration in 1912, war-time legislation such as the Military Service Act and the Defence of the Realm Act prevented the South Wales men from acting similarly. Tillett's organisation therefore benefited significantly from registration. How far registration was to provide a basis for decasualisation after the war, on the other hand, is another matter.

Recruitment from industry, 1914-1918

During the war the Dockers' Union increased its membership in manufacturing industries as well as on the waterfront. As strikes were made illegal, a large number of workers found that they needed good representation at arbitration proceedings, and thus joined it and other general unions. In South Wales Dockers' officials enrolled quarrymen, dock pilots and women munition workers at Newport; girl toy-makers, Woolworth's shop assistants, brewery workers, stocking factory girls and munition workers at Swansea; flannel and woollen workers, and agricultural labourers in West Wales; men and women at forge and munition works in the Port Talbot district; and patent fuel workers and canal bargemen at Cardiff. After 1914 the N.A.L.U. also grew by recruiting dock pilots, gasworkers, ships' storemen and insurance agents within the region. The Cardiff Coal Trimmers' Association, however, still concentrated upon its coal trimming membership at the docks: its strength declined from 2,050 in 1914 to 1,899 in 1918, as some members were killed in battle.

Although several general unions enrolled workers in South Wales after 1914, there were few inter-union disputes. As it was war-time Dockers' officials largely co-operated with these organisations. The Dockers' leaders also tried to maintain good relations with the employers, but they were unable to prevent some of their new recruits from leaving work unofficially. For instance, women munition workers at the National Cartridge and Box Repair Factory in Newport struck in June 1917 after the management had stopped the supply of hot water for making tea, and six months later walked out again following an alteration in their hours of work. In addition, labourers at the North Central Waggon Works in Port Talbot struck unofficially for union recognition in May 1918. Yet these disputes did not disrupt production for long, and were not as serious as those in the mining and engineering industries.

Dockers' officials also attempted to discourage those workers they had organised before 1914 from striking. Aware of how effective the Tinplate Conciliation Board had been in preventing stoppages before the war, they eventually managed to establish conciliation boards in other industries. In March 1918 the Copper Trade Conciliation Board was revised to represent workmen and employers from the copper, yellow metal and chemical industries of South Wales, and several months later a Galvanising Conciliation Board was formed. At the same time Dockers' leaders also tried to preserve good relations with the tinplate companies by agreeing in 1914 that no new demands were to be made by either side and that outstanding claims were to remain in abeyance during the war. Union representatives claimed that this arrangement was made because they believed that the war would not continue for long, but it must be seen as another instance of the Dockers' reluctance to press the demands of their tinplate members very strongly. The Dockers' pact, nonetheless, was soon broken by the unofficial action of its rank and file.

In January 1915 the Government took over the tinplate works of South Wales and Monmouthshire as controlled establishments in order to ensure adequate supplies of steel to the armament industry. The supply of steel to the tinplate industry was reduced, and tinplate companies were forced to cut their output. Some tinplate workers were made redundant and had to obtain employment elsewhere, but this did not prevent those who remained in the industry from achieving wage improvements. As the price of tinplates was rising, tinplate workers with low incomes were able to gain a war bonus in March 1915 from the Conciliation Board. Other men in the industry, though, were not granted an increase, and, despite the opposition of their union officials to strikes, began militant action. In May 1915 boiler firemen at five tinplate works in Llanelly struck without union approval for three days, and resumed only after Wignall and Pugh, the district secretary, had advised them to allow the issue to be settled by the Conciliation Board. Because of the success of 200,000 South Wales miners in July 1915 in winning increases by strike action, workers in the tinplate trade continued to demand more pay. They asked their employers for an advance of 15%, and a meeting was called in October to discuss the claim. Eventually wage increases were agreed: workers earning less than 20/- a week were given 15% war bonus; from 20/- to 30/-, 20%; from 30/- to 40/-, 15%; from 40/- upwards, 10%. Following a growth in demand for tinplates during the early months of 1916, a further advance was given in June 1916.

In spite of the failure of Dockers' officials to press the tinplate workers' demands, the men remained loyal to their organisation. Although the tinplate workmen were invited in 1916 to join the Iron and Steel Confederation, a body established by unions in the iron and steel trades to prevent inter-union disputes, they declined to do so. A special conference held at Swansea to consider this question decided by 65 votes to 4 to reject the proposed scheme of amalgamation. To some extent the tinplate workers were influenced by the Dockers' leaders who did not encourage the scheme. As the Dockers' Union was a general union, amalgamation would have led to the complete severance of the tinplate branches. The tinplate section was the third largest district of the organisation, and the Dockers' executive did not wish to lose it: in 1915 the union's income had been £36,353, of which the tinplate workers had contributed £3,399. Yet other reasons also explain why these men remained in Tillett's union. In the first place, Dockers' officials had helped to reduce distress in the tinplate district at the beginning of the war. Secondly, the tinplate workers probably felt that their position in the works would be best safeguarded by their present representatives. Following the removal of the tinplate industry from the Reserved Occupations List in January 1916, the Conciliation Board agreed that er 'oyers had the right if shortages of labour occurred to request workmen to work in a grade other than their own, and that the men would not incur wage-cuts as a result. As experienced union negotiators were needed to supervise these procedures, the tinplate workers decided to retain their existing leaders. Finally, they lacked any assurance that they would gain autonomy in the Confederation and that their opinions would not be stifled by the millmen; at least in the Dockers' Union they had their own district representatives.

The removal of the tinplate industry from the list of reserved occupations led to a considerable reduction in its labour force. In 1913 there had been 28,000 workers in the trade; in 1918 there were 15,100. Many were conscripted into the Army or were transferred to steel and spelter works to perform tasks of national importance. To ensure that enough workers were left to man the tinplate mills, a central committee was formed in 1917 by the Ministry of Labour, the Ministry of Munitions, the War Office, the companies and those unions with members at tinplate works. Local committees were also created at each works by employers and union officials in order to report to the central committee the number of men who could be spared and to refer all disputes to it. The Dockers' Union played an important part in the establishment and administration of these bodies.

As the price of tinplates remained at a high level, those workmen who remained in the industry were able to gain further wage improvements. In May 1917 the tinplate workers demanded an increase of 25%, and a special meeting of the Tinplate Conciliation Board was called to discuss the issue. Tillett represented the men, and negotiated a settlement: workers earning less than 20/- a week gained 15%; between 20/- and 30/-, 20%; between 30/- and 40/-, 20%, and over 40/- per week, 15%. Yet the men were not completely satisfied with Tillett's efforts, and in June 1917 they obtained an additional 5% war bonus and put forward a new claim for a 40% increase. Their demands were again considered by the Conciliation Board, though on this occasion the employers and union representatives could not agree and passed the matter to a government body, the Committee on Production. The Committee awarded the tinplate workers 5/- per week, but its decision was considerably opposed by the lowest paid workmen. Strike notices were handed in at a number of works, and a new claim was submitted to the firms. Eventually an agreement was achieved in July 1918 when the following settlement was drawn up.

Wage-rates in June 1918		New rate (as from 14th July 1918)	
	%		%
Earnings up to per week	increase on 1914	Earnings up to per week increase	increase on 1914
20/-	52½	10	62½
20/1 to 30/-	72½	22½	95
30/1 to 40/-	67½	17½	85
40/1 to 50/-	62½	12½	75
50/1 to 60/-	60	10	70
60/1 to 70/-	50	5	55
70/1 to 100/-	42½	2½	45
100/1 and upwards	40	2½	42½

Table 7

Some of these improvements, particularly those negotiated for lower-paid workmen, compare favourably with the percentage increases obtained by port workers during this period. Nevertheless, it must not be forgotten that port workers obtained many additional payments after 1914, and their overtime rates were high.

The development of the Dockers' Union in industry after the War

Following the Armistice, the Government repealed the compulsory arbitration clauses of the Munitions Acts and removed other restrictions. It hoped that employers and unions would improve their relations and would prevent industry from being disrupted. It had set an example to them by establishing the Whitley Committee in 1917 to consider the organisation of industrial relations after the war. This Committee had recommended the formation of Joint Industrial Councils at a national and local level, and had advised that they should be used to discuss wages, conditions and problems concerning industrial efficiency and management. Even though the Committee's proposals were later rejected by a number of unions, they were supported by the Dockers' Union whose officials continued to prefer to settle disputes by conciliation rather than by strike action.

In several industries where the Dockers had members, Joint Industrial Councils were established. The tinplate industry, for instance, formed such a body in March 1919. At a meeting in Swansea tinplate employers and unions agreed that a Joint Industrial Council would replace the Conciliation Board, and consist of 32 representatives of the Welsh Plate Association and 32 representatives of the workmen's organisations. It was also decided that this body would meet six times a year and that one of these discussions would be used to examine the position of trade, technical developments, government legislation affecting the trade, and the welfare of tinplate workers. Although the Joint Industrial Council debated wider issues than the Conciliation Board had done, few constitutional changes were needed to bring the latter into line with the recommendations of the Whitley Committee. In fact, it has been claimed that the constitution of the Conciliation Board of the tinplate industry was taken as a model by the Whitley Committee.

Between 1919-1920 the tinplate industry expanded as did most industries. The price of tinplate rose from 32/- per box in June 1919 to 41/- in January 1920, and by April 1920 had risen to 72/-. The growth of the industry encouraged the tinplate workers to demand another advancement in wages. At first the employers resisted, but in June 1919 they agreed to increase the war bonus by 12½%. In January 1920 a further war bonus of 40% was conceded, and three months later this was increased to 50%. Such large concessions were made because trade was booming and firms wished to avoid a dispute. As a result the men took full advantage of their strong bargaining position, and in June 1920 persuaded the companies to hire extra men in the mills to reduce their work-load, and asked the Joint Industrial Council to change the system of payment in the industry. The tinplate workers demanded that price-rates should be based on weight rather than on area, and that a sliding-scale should be introduced as an addition to the basic rates. The employers rejected the men's claim for a tonnage rate, but they agreed in January 1921 to introduce a sliding-scale based upon the price per ton of tinplate bars. This acted as a supplement to the basic wage-scale which was fixed at 25% higher than the old scale, the "1874 list".

After 1918 wage improvements were also achieved by Dockers' members in other South Wales industries. Some of these were negotiated on a national basis by the N.T.W.F., for Ernest Bevin was strongly convinced of the value of national wage agreements. In October 1918 advances of 5/- per week were obtained for workers in the engineering and foundry, soap and candle, explosives, ship-building, chemical and clay industries, and in 1919 road transport workmen gained 4/- per week increase. Local agreements, too, were successfully concluded by union representatives for workers in the chemical, copper, brewery, woollen, cotton and patent fuel industries, and for council workmen and powerhouse men. The Dockers' Union also negotiated a reduction of hours for millers, confectionary workers and men in the seed crushing industry, and in 1919 the 48 hour week for carters and motormen was introduced.

Although most of these increases were obtained without the use of industrial action, some strikes did occur. But, as on the waterfront, the union was largely implicated not out of its own choosing. At Swansea, for instance, the local tramwaymen struck in April 1920 for higher wages in spite of the N.T.W.F.'s negotiation of a national award of 6/- per week for them several days previously. Similar disputes also arose in Manchester, Oldham, Huddersfield, Cardiff and Llanelly, but the workers involved did not achieve very much. The Dockers' Union refused to support their action, for its leaders believed that the men should respect agreements and that stoppages should be called only after all attempts at conciliation had failed. They especially did not want to anger employers unnecessarily, and jeopardise the existence of the Joint Industrial Councils upon which the union had representation. Tillett's organisation, nevertheless, did not advocate peace at any price. When it felt that industrial action was justified, it backed its members' demands forcefully. In particular the union vigorously opposed firms which refused to recognise it or which victimised its rank and file.

In spite of the large amount of strike benefit the union was forced to pay to members throughout Britain during this period, its assets grew because of an increase in membership. Most of its existing branches expanded, and new ones were opened. During 1919 and 1920 toy-makers at Cardiff, chemical workers at Newport and Swansea, fuel workers at Port Talbot, and salmon fishermen at St. Dogmaels were enrolled. In the summer of 1920, however, recruitment was halted as the post-war boom broke. Prices fell, unemployment increased, and wages were reduced in most industries, including the tinplate trade because of a decline in the price of tinplate bars. Some trade unionists in the lead and woollen industries bitterly rejected wage decreases and were eventually locked-out by their companies, but these workmen did not do any better than those who did not resist. The Dockers' Union realised this; although it negotiated on behalf of its members, it did not advise prolonged hostility towards reductions. No doubt its leaders remembered their costly confrontations during earlier recessions, especially 1891, and were considerably influenced by the defeats of unions such as the Miners which had opposed cuts.

During 1921, because of the decline of trade and a rise in unemployment, the membership of many Dockers' branches decreased. At Swansea district contributions fell from £6,805 to £4,974, at Cardiff from £6,181 to £3,724, at Port Talbot from £5,431 to £3,278, at Newport from £4,096 to £3,285, and at Barry from £2,944 to £2,003. Yet, although the Dockers' strength was undermined, its officials had adopted a realistic policy during negotiations with the employers. If the union had firmly resisted wage reductions and had been humiliated in the process, its assets would have fallen substantially and its membership might have diminished even more than it did. Such a policy was also adopted at the ports, and it is the union's attitude towards wages and registration on the waterfront that we must now closely examine.

Unionism at the ports, 1919-1921

During the war registration had been introduced at the docks of South Wales to ensure that an adequate supply of labour was available while army recruitment was in progress. After demobilisation, because of the influx of labour to the waterfront, the Port Labour Committees remained in existence in order to preserve the industry for the regular worker. In November 1918 a meeting of their representatives at London decided that these bodies would deal with the question of employment at the ports, that their constitutions would be amended so as to secure equal representation of employers and employed, and that a Central Advisory Committee consisting of twelve representatives of companies and twelve of labour would be set up to co-ordinate their work and to advise the Ministry of Labour. The Central Advisory Committee also tried subsequently to persuade ports which had not registered dock labour to do so, and in February 1919 it sent a "model scheme" dealing with the employment of waterside workers to all ports as a basis for discussion. The scheme recommended that bona fide workers should be registered by local Port Labour Committees, that they should receive a metal tally from the employment exchange, and that they should produce this tally in order to be hired. The Central Advisory Committee, though, lacked any powers to enforce its suggestions. Whereas a number of ports improved their systems of registration, others rejected the Committee's advice. Furthermore, registration did not operate as efficiently as it could have done, because it was exploited by the unions to increase their memberships, and largely failed to deal with the problem of the over-supply of labour.

At Swansea the war-time system of registration was improved upon, but at Cardiff and Newport registration was misused. At Cardiff the Central Advisory Committee's suggestions for reform were rejected, and registration was later moved from the direct control of the Port Labour Committee. It was arranged that the unions themselves would issue registration cards, with the result that the Port Labour Committee gradually ceased to have any knowledge of the number of men on the register. The procedure became little more than an undertaking by companies to engage only trade unionists, and completely failed to reduce underemployment. At Newport registration was used by the National Amalgamated Labourers' Union as a means to boost its membership at the expense of the Dockers' Union. The N.A.L.U. gave Port Labour cards to all new recruits, even if they had not previously worked on the waterside. Nonetheless, Dockers' officials such as Henry Seer (nick-named "Half-way Harry" by the rank and file because of his willingness to compromise) did not firmly oppose this move, and tried to settle their difficulties with the N.A.L.U. peacefully. Their members at the port, on the other hand, strongly criticised the N.A.L.U.'s policies, for competition at the hiring-centres was intensified. A local syndicalist, Frank Kendall, was thus able to gain considerable backing for his proposal to take over the work of the Port Labour Committee. According to Kendall, he called a mass meeting of dockers in June 1919 at the Gem Cinema, Newport, where it was unanimously agreed that a new body, the Joint Committee, would be formed. Kendall and eleven other militants were voted onto the committee, and were known thereafter as "Tom Mann's dozen" because of their syndicalist views. Not only did they control the distribution of Port Labour cards, but they also took over the management of industrial disputes. At the meeting Kendall had shrewdly introduced a resolution giving his new committee the power to call a strike. The Joint Committee survived until February 1920 when it was forced to dissolve. Kendall had gone to Llandrindod Wells to convalesce after a serious attack of rheumatic fever, and Seer, O'Leary, Lynch, Screen and other local officials used this opportunity to arrange another meeting and regain their control. This time they did not abuse it and did not sacrifice the employment situation of the dockers by increasing their membership at the waterside, but they do not appear to have introduced any effective means of limiting the size of the labour force. The number of labourers at the port of Newport remained far in excess of that required to meet normal demands.

Despite the many disadvantages of the casual hiring system, Dockers' leaders such as Ernest Bevin failed to persuade employers and workmen to accept decasualisation, nor did they gain much support from the Government. The Shaw Inquiry of 1920, which was set up to examine port workers' wages, criticised the system of employment on the waterfront, but no reforms were immediately introduced. The casual hiring system remained, and continued to affect industrial relations at the ports. Although the conflict between the union and companies over the closed shop issue had largely come to an end during the First World War, differences over wages, hours and methods of hiring still arose because of the method of employment. According to Lascelles and Bullock,

> The casual hiring system has produced a tradition of ill-will and suspicion which it may be difficult to wipe out while the system lasts . . . The system of casual employment seems designed to destroy all feeling of responsibility between employers and men, and to bring out every instinct of antagonism and distrust.[6]

In spite of the demobilisation of the troops after the First World War, unemployment did not increase very much. A heavy demand for industrial goods arose and led to a growth of trade during 1919. As a result of these developments and the greater bargaining power of the port workers brought about by registration, the Dockers' Union pressed for wage advances and a reduction of hours. The union's demands were forwarded by the National Transport Workers' Federation which had become prominent during the war.

The National Transport Workers' Federation achieved two important settlements after 1918 : the 44 hour working week agreement and the Shaw Award. The first of these recommended in March 1919 the adoption of a 44 hour working week at all ports and the introduction of a minimum engagement period of half a day. The Shaw Award of March 1920 led to wage increases for dock labourers throughout the country, and was brought about by the Federation's demand for a national minimum of 16/- a day for workers on the waterfront. When this claim was initially submitted to the employers, they suggested that it should be examined at a public court of enquiry to be appointed by the Ministry of Labour under the Industrial Courts Act of 1919. In spite of the successful strikes undertaken by railwaymen and other trade unionists in 1919, Bevin accepted their proposal, and in February 1920 he presented the dock workers' case to the Court. At these proceedings Bevin argued that wages at the waterside had fallen in relation to the cost of living especially since 1914, and that the ship-owners, dock authorities and merchants could afford to pay increases out of the large profits they had made during the war. Although the employers backed their case strongly, they could not match Bevin's arguments and enthusiasm. The port workers' claim was granted in full, and Bevin was known thereafter as "the dockers' K.C.".

The coal trimmers also made a number of important gains during this period. In February 1920 a Court of Enquiry appointed by the Ministry of Labour to consider the question of the hours and conditions of workmen employed for the tipping and trimming of coal met at Cardiff. The Court was set up to examine the men's request that they should work only two shifts and that night-work should be stopped. Their demand was conceded, though the Court ruled that the employers could enforce night-work if trade warranted it. In June 1920 they achieved a further wage increase when a Joint Conference of the Shipping Federation, the South Wales Trimming Board and representatives of the N.T.W.F. agreed that the rates for loading coal would be increased and that trimmers would receive many 'extras' for special work.

The N.T.W.F. obtained these significant gains for its members without using strike action. Although 61 million working days were lost through disputes in 1919 and 1920, during that time the Federation was not involved in a single major stoppage. Its attitude did not change even when the employers demanded wage reductions following the decline of trade after September 1920. With the growth of unemployment the N.T.W.F.'s leaders realised that a strike on the waterfront could be broken by firms using blackleg labour, and they did not wish to jeopardise the existence of the National Council which was established with the port employers for national bargaining purposes in December 1920. The "Black Friday" incident in April 1921, when they and the railwaymen's officials decided not to support the miners over the issue of wage cuts in the mining industry, also emphasised to them the futility of confrontation during the depression. The N.T.W.F. therefore accepted reductions as the only alternative. Following negotiations with the companies it was agreed that wage decreases of 2/- a day for labourers at the principal ports of the country would come into force from 4th August, 1921, and that a further reduction of 1/- a day would take effect from 5th January, 1922. The wages of coal trimmers were also cut by 10% from 16th August, 1921.

The N.T.W.F.'s attitude towards industrial action was not fully accepted by the Dockers' rank and file. Though there were few strikes during 1921 because of the decline of trade, many local disputes occurred in 1919 and 1920 over wage-rates, hiring conditions and other issues. At Swansea the employers regarded their workmen's claims for "extras" as so excessive that they locked out a thousand of them in April 1919. The men were out of work for a month before the companies agreed to meet Dockers' officials. A conference was finally held at the Ministry of Labour in London where it was decided that work would be immediately resumed on the same basis as before the stoppage and that a new tariff for the port would be formulated. A year later another serious dispute occurred at Swansea over wages. In spite of the Shaw Inquiry's approval of the N.T.W.F.'s claim for a 16/- per day minimum for dock labourers throughout the country, 5000 Swansea port workers stopped work in August 1920 for a guinea per day. But they received no support from their representatives, and were forced to abandon their demand.

Strikes also took place at Cardiff and Newport over wages and conditions on the waterfront. At Cardiff the pitwood workers struck in August 1920, and at Newport the cargo workers influenced by Frank Kendall and Alfred Cox left work frequently. Cox, in addition, continued his bitter dispute with Houlder Brothers. Despite the attempts of the N.T.W.F. to settle this issue, Houlders' ships were still "blacked" after the First World War at Newport docks. Nevertheless, Houlders solved their problem in 1919 by offering the post of chief foreman to Cox. Cox accepted their offer, but only after he had gained the full approval of the men at a mass meeting. Thereafter he used his position to operate the closed shop and to give employment to militants such as Kendall who found difficulty in obtaining work at the port.

Finally, some disputes involved the Dockers' efforts to enforce a union monopoly at various hiring centres. At Barry in January 1920 dock masters' staff, tugboatmen, gatemen, general cargo and pitwood workers left work unofficially because two members of the National Union of Railwaymen were employed by the Barry Railway Company on the dock masters' staff. The strikers requested that the two men should be transferred to another department and that other members of the dock masters' staff who had joined the N.U.R. should hold a Dockers' Union card. The power of the men's organisation was such that the company capitulated after two days and granted their demands in full.

Although Tillett's union had grown considerably during the war (its annual income increased from £29,677 in 1914 to £87,075 in 1918), attempts were subsequently made to strengthen it even further. In 1918 a scheme was formulated to amalgamate the Dockers and the National Union of General

Workers. Yet, when a ballot was taken on the issue, an insufficient number of the Dockers' rank and file voted, because they were discouraged by officials such as Bevin who did not favour it. The scheme was not revived. Bevin, however, persisted with his own plans, and eventually tried to forge an amalgamation among waterfront organisations. In August 1920 a conference of thirteen waterside unions including the Dockers' Union, the N.A.L.U. and the Cardiff, Penarth and Barry Coal Trimmers' Union was held at London. Influenced considerably by the development of national wage negotiations for the port industry since 1918, these bodies unanimously supported amalgamation and set up a committee consisting of one representative from each organisation to devise how it would be achieved. Before this scheme was prepared, Bevin also invited seven road transport workers' unions to join in the discussions. Six of these accepted, and they played an important part. In December 1920 a draft constitution was completed, and was approved by leaders of nineteen unions who agreed to persuade their members to back it.

The proposals involved the amalgamation of these unions to form a new organisation, the Transport and General Workers' Union, which was to consist of five trade groups for the dockers, waterway employees, clerical and administrative workers, road transport workers and general workers. These trade groups were to be given their own executives and national organisations, were to be largely autonomous, and were to make their own claims and to negotiate with employers. For administrative purposes, the Transport and General Workers' Union was to be divided into eleven regions with one representative from each on the General Executive Council. Each national trade group was also allocated one representative upon the General Executive Council which was to have control over the funds and the sole power to declare a strike. Such a constitution was devised to ensure that established leaders in the existing unions would retain their influence in the new organisation, and to prevent workers from losing their sense of identity.

The unions which helped to draft the constitution held a ballot amongst their members, and fourteen decided to amalgamate, including the Dockers and the N.A.L.U. The Cardiff Coal Trimmers' Association and four other organisations, however, voted against amalgamation. Although the Coal Trimmers' Executive Committee favoured the scheme, their members probably felt that their monopoly at the hiring-centres would be undermined if they accepted it. Nonetheless, the fourteen unions went ahead with their proposals, and in May 1921 set up a Provisional Executive Council. The elected Provisional Executive Officers were Harry Gosling, the President; Ernest Bevin, the General Secretary; and H. W. Kay, the Provisional Treasurer. On January 1st, 1922 their powers became official, and the mighty Transport and General Workers' Union came into existence.

The amalgamation of these organisations led Will Judge, a Dockers' official, to stress the improvement of conditions on the waterfront since 1889.

1889 and 1921! What dates to conjure with! Those few of us who are left, the pioneers of the greatest movement in Labour's history, must very often look back with astonishment mingled with pride as we recall the struggle of '89. Let us never forget the damnable conditions of our employment, where men were hired like slaves in an Eastern slave market, treated worse than beasts, injured and murdered - yes, murdered - and daily robbed of their earnings, and their very manhood sapped by the hired bullies and cosh-carriers, who were the recognised gangers of a bad and corrupt body, men without souls whose lust and greed caused them to ignore the traffic in human flesh and blood and to only concern themselves about securing dividends and profits for their shareholders. Thank God those bad old days have passed.[7]

Judge could also have pointed out that wages had improved and that many port labourers in South Wales and elsewhere had achieved and benefited from the closed shop. On the other hand, the calling-on system remained, the men's employment was still irregular and industrial disputes continued to occur because of the method of hiring. Dockers' officials had found it very difficult to improve this situation, for decasualisation had been rejected by the employers and the rank and file. By 1921 all they could do was to hope that the T.G.W.U. would find a solution:

If the casual labour question is to be solved satisfactorily a good deal of patience and hard work will be necessary on the part of those responsible for the scheme. In addition great educational work is necessary, and self-discipline on the part of the men is required to enable the scheme to work satisfactorily.[8]

NOTES

1. *Dockers' Record,* January, 1916, p.5.
2. Ibid., October, 1915, p.7.
3. *Enquiry into the Wages and Conditions of Employment of Dock and Waterside Labourers* (1920), Cmd. 937, Volume II, p.171.
4. *Dockers' Record,* May, 1918, p.3.
5. Ibid., August, 1918, p.10.
6. E.C.P. Lascelles and S.S. Bullock, *Dock Labour and Decasualisation,* London, 1924, pp.169-170.
7. *Dockers' Record,* June-July, 1921, p.6.
8. *The Record,* August, 1921, p.4.

Chapter 5
Conclusion

Conclusion

At the ports of South Wales the casual hiring system affected relations between regular port workers and employers more than any other factor, for competition from outsiders at the hiring-centres led the Dockers' Union and local waterfront unions to try to enforce the closed shop. Only by gaining preference of employment could they effectively obtain a greater amount of work for their members, raise the level of wages and obtain stable memberships. Tillett and Mann initially believed that this would be easily achieved, as they considered it to be in the firms' interests to engage only their members. Yet they were very mistaken. Most companies opposed the Dockers' demands because they found that a union monopoly led to inefficiency and weakened their bargaining position. Although some were prepared to give preference of employment to skilled groups such as coal trimmers, they were unwilling to hire general labourers on this basis. The issue was not easily resolved, and a number of bitter disputes were fought over the closed shop before 1914. Only during the First World War, when registration schemes were introduced, was the problem finally concluded.

The casual hiring system influenced not only the earning capacity of the port worker but also his social behaviour. Violence, volatility, fearfulness of change and distrustfulness of authority were, as Charles Booth has described in *Life and Labour of the People in London,* distinctive characteristics of the port labourer, and were closely related to the method of employment in dockland. In no other industry in which the Dockers' Union recruited members were men as violent and as strike-orientated as the dockers, or gain such independent power as militants such as Cox and Kendall. However, this is not to argue that the attitudes of port workers contributed positively towards the development of trade unionism at the waterside. In 1891 and 1892 Tillett's union was involved in expensive confrontations because of the unofficial action of the Cardiff coal tippers and Swansea dock labourers, and suffered humiliating defeats. Casual employment also led to sectionalism amongst the waterfront labour force. Some workers with particular skills such as coal trimmers did not affiliate to the same organisation as general dock labourers, because they wished to emphasise their own skills and because they believed that the encroachment of labourers at their calling-on stands would be best prevented by belonging to a different union. The Swansea coal trimmers, for instance, remained in the N.A.L.U. in 1890 despite the desertion of fellow workmen to Tillett's union; the Newport coal trimmers joined the Dockers, although the riverside workers had affiliated to the N.A.L.U; the Cardiff, Barry and Penarth coal trimmers formed a separate organisation, the Cardiff, Penarth and Barry Coal Trimmers' Association. The aloofness of the Cardiff Coal Trimmers' Association affected the development of the Dockers' Union in Cardiff, because during the 1891 and 1911 dock disputes its policies undermined the position of workers on strike.

Although the trade cycle influenced the bargaining strength of the

Dockers' Union and dictated when its members could move from attack to defence, it did not determine whether it survived or not. The survival of the Dockers' Union at its various strongholds in South Wales instead depended mainly upon the attitude of the employer. At Newport the Alexandra (Newport and South Wales) Docks and Railway Company declined to spend its capital upon crushing the Dockers' Union and recognised it. The company preferred to pay high wages rather than incur lengthy stoppages and risk losing trade to nearby Bristol Channel ports. At Cardiff, on the other hand, the powerful Bute Docks Company (later renamed the Cardiff Railway Company) was totally opposed to mass unionism on the waterfront. It refused to recognise the Dockers' Union until 1915, and so did prominent port employers, such as the timber merchants. Following its defeat at Cardiff in 1891 the union was able to regain a foothold there only in 1911, when a period of prolonged trade expansion occurred.

The hostility of firms to the closed shop and the fluctuation of trade caused the Dockers' Union to be a most unstable body. In 1890 and 1911 the union was a mass organisation; in the interim period it was forced to rely upon the support of groups of waterfront workers who had gained preference of employment. This instability led the Dockers' officials to attempt to improve their position in several ways. Even though the union had originally been largely concerned with the organisation of port labourers, its officials later recruited tinplate and industrial workers in order to obtain levies and regular contributions when strikes affected the waterside. A tinplate district was opened in West Wales, and branches were established at copper, lead and galvanising works. Dockers' officials also tried to increase the port workers' influence by forming federations with other organisations. In 1890 a small federation was initiated in South Wales with the Sailors, Riggers and the N.A.L.U; in 1891 it was enlarged to form the South Wales and Monmouthshire Federation of Trades and Labour Unions; and in 1910 the National Transport Workers' Federation was created. But these federations were themselves weak in some respects: demarcation disputes occurred, especially between the Dockers and the N.A.L.U., and the federations were unable to prevent the Dockers from suffering heavy defeats at the hands of the employers. It was therefore gradually realised that amalgamation was the only effective solution.

Although the Dockers' Union was formed as a result of the London dock strike and was subsequently involved in strikes on the waterfront, its leaders preferred to settle disputes without the use of strike action. Despite Tillett's eloquent speeches on behalf of the port workers, the Dockers' General Secretary was not really so militant as he appeared. Tillett rarely caused a strike himself, supported conciliation, and believed that only by offering a guarantee of efficient and uninterrupted work to concerns could he persuade them to give preference of employment to his members. Many of the Dockers' rank and file, however, disliked such an attitude, and often struck without obtaining the permission of their union officials who, they felt, were too moderate and slow to investigate complaints. Yet few of them were revolutionaries, for they struck largely for increased wages and the closed shop. Even though syndicalists such as Alf Cox and George Jackson won much support after 1910, they were thanked by the men not for their revolutionary outbursts but for their help in conducting disputes and promoting wage demands.

As the Dockers' Union did not back some of the men's unofficial stoppages, it is questionable how much the port labourers and industrial workers benefited by belonging to the organisation. In the first place, waterfront labourers did not have to be members of the Dockers' Union to obtain wage increases; in 1897 and 1911 non-unionists gained improved rates of pay following strike action. Unionists, too, were successful in many strikes without the financial assistance of their Executive Council. In the second place, Tillett and his officials did little to help the tinplate workers increase their wages. In spite of the expansion of the tinplate industry after 1900 the workmen's demands were not pressed very strongly, because Tillett wished to confine industrial conflict to the waterside. Nevertheless, regular port workers certainly benefited from the reputation, oratorical powers and experience of their leaders during some disputes. They also gained much from the Dockers' enforcement of the closed shop which strengthened their bargaining position and gave them more security of employment. But the union was unable to persuade all port workers that this was so; a number of men remained in the N.A.L.U. after 1890 because they thought that a different ticket would give them greater job security.

John Lovell in a study of trade unionism at the port of London between 1870 and 1914 concluded that the casual hiring system lies at the root of the institutional weakness of waterside organisation.[1] His analysis applies equally well to South Wales as it does to London. Both in London and the provinces workers joined different societies, bitter disputes were fought over the closed shop issue, and instability of organisation existed. Yet, although the casual hiring system was in many ways unsatisfactory, it remained in existence at the major ports until the late 1960's. Firms supported this method of employment because, due to fluctuations of trade, it was more economical; port workers approved because they were fearful of change and because they felt it gave them more independence. The persistence of the casual hiring system meant that the attitudes of the men were perpetuated. Workers on the waterfront thus remained reluctant to obey officials and continued to leave work without permission. As the Devlin Inquiry of 1965 argued,

> It would indeed be surprising if the casual system of employment in the docks did not induce a more irresponsible attitude than that in industry generally. Casual labour produces a casual attitude. If the employer does not provide work unless he wants to, why should the employee go to work unless he wants to? If a man is used to having work one day and

none the next, is there anything very wrong about taking a day off on his own choice, whether for his own pleasure or to air a grievance by a token strike?[2]

NOTES

1. J. Lovell, *Stevedores and Dockers,* London, 1969.
2. *Final Report of the Committee of Inquiry under the Rt. Hon. Lord Devlin into certain matters concerning the Port Transport Industry,* Cmd. 2734, London, 1965.

17. A group of frightened Chinese are protected by Cardiff policemen in Bute Street, Cardiff, during the dock strikes of 1911

18. The morning after . . . A Chinese laundry in Mackintosh Place, Cardiff, wrecked by rioters in July 1911

19. We've won! This photograph clearly shows the delight on the faces of a group of Cardiff dockers and seamen when it was announced that their employers had agreed to grant increases in July 1911

20. Enforcement of the closed-shop at Newport Docks by the coal trimmers and tippers in 1913

21. Frank Kendall, the founder of the Joint Committee, in Newport in June 1919.

22. A view of the Melingriffith Tinplate Works, Whitchurch, Cardiff, taken before the First World War

23. A rollerman entering a "piece of singles" into rolls at the Clayton Tinplate Works, Pontardulais, Glamorgan (formerly known as the Pontardulais Tinplate Works). In the picture, too, is a behinder receiving it from him

24. A doubler in the process of doubling a sheet at the Clayton Tinplate Works, Glamorgan

25. A shearer at work with crocodile shears, with a bundler handing over the pieces at the Clayton Tinplate Works, Glamorgan

Appendices

Appendix 1

Table showing Average Retail Prices, Average Money Prices and Percentage Unemployed, 1889-1914.

	(a) Average Retail Prices (1850 = 100)	(b) Average Money Wages (1850 = 100)	(c) Percentage Unemployed
1889	91	156	2.1
1890	91	163	2.1
1891	92	163	3.5
1892	92	162	6.3
1893	89	162	7.5
1894	87	162	6.9
1895	84	162	5.8
1896	83	163	3.3
1897	86	166	3.3
1898	87	167	2.8
1899	86	172	2.0
1900	89	179	2.5
1901	90	179	3.3
1902	91	176	4.0
1903	92	174	4.7
1904	93	173	6.0
1905	92	174	5.0
1906	92	176	3.6
1907	95	182	3.7
1908	97	181	7.8
1909	97	179	7.7
1910	98	179½	4.7
1911	99	179	3.0
1912	103	184	3.2
1913	103	188½	2.1
1914	102	189½	3.3

Sources: Column (a) and (b) - W. T. Layton and G. Crowther, *Introduction to the Study of Prices,* London, 1938, p.274.

Column (c) - *Fifteenth Abstract of Labour Statistics,* Cs 6228, 1912, p.6; London and Cambridge Economic Service, *The British Economy: Key Statistics 1900-1966,* London, 1967.

Appendix 2

Income of the Dockers' Union in half-yearly periods in the Newport, Cardiff, Barry, Port Talbot and Swansea areas, 1890-1921. The graph also shows the income of the Dockers' tinplate district which was formed in 1908. (District incomes include the contributions of port workers and workers in other industries).

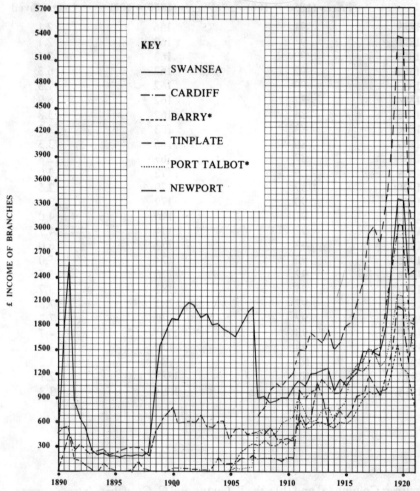

KEY

——— SWANSEA

—·— CARDIFF

------ BARRY*

— — TINPLATE

·········· PORT TALBOT*

——– NEWPORT

£ INCOME OF BRANCHES

To avoid confusion with the Cardiff contributions, Port Talbot and Barry have not been included on the graph until 1905.

*In 1908 the Port Talbot area became a separate district of the Dockers' Union. It consisted of the Port Talbot dockers and several branches of copper workers previously organised in the Swansea district.

Appendix 3

Rates for shipping general goods at Newport in 1915.

Per Ton

Angle Iron	5d.
Ammonia, in bags	6d.
Ammonia, overside from Craft	8d.
Anchors and Chains	4½d.
Axles and Wheels	3½d.
Billets	4¾d.
Bricks (Fire and Furnace) loose	7d.
Bridge Work	6d.
Beer in Barrels	4½d.
Buckets (weight)	1/0
Blooms	4½d.
Bloom Ends	4½d.
Boiler Plates	6d.
Black Steel Sheets	7d.
Barrell Staves	1/0
Bags in Bales	1/0
Barbed Wire	1/0
Channels - Short lengths	5d.
Channels - Long lengths or mixed	6d.
Cement - Packed in Casks or Cases, as General Goods	5d.
Cement - Packed in Bags	6d.
Coal - (Small) in Bags	7d.
Coal - (Large) in Bags	8d.
Coke in Bags	11d.
Cast Iron Pipes	4½d.
Cobbles and Old Wire	6d.
Carriage and Wagon Work	6d.
Crossings and Points	6d.
Earthenware Pipes (weight)	1/0
Galvanised Iron (flat), in Bundles	5d.
Galvanised Iron (all other, in Cases or Bundles)	3½d.
General Goods	5d.
General Light Class Goods from Carts and Railway Lorries	1/0
Hay in Bales	7d.
Horse Shoes, loose	10d.
Hoop Iron	5d.
Iron Rods, long, twisted, over 50ft. in length	1/0
Machinery	6d.
Nail Rods	5d.
Oil in Barrels	4½d.
Pipes, Cast-Iron	4½d.
Pipes, Earthenware (weight)	1/0

Patent Manure, packed in Casks or Cases, as General Goods .... 5d.
Pig Iron .... 5d.
Points and Crossings .... 6d.
Rails (old), Contractor's Plant .... 5d.
Rails (old), off Bank .... 5½d.
Shovels (weight) 1/0
Spelter, in Casks or loose .... 4½d.
All Spiegel Iron, in Casks or loose .... 4½d.
Scrap Iron, loose .... 6½d.
Scrap Iron, under ⅜in in thickness .... 9d.
Scrap Iron, ⅜in and over in thickness .... 6½d.
Scrap Iron, in Blocks, such as Rolls, etc. 4d
Smiths' Iron .... 6d.
Standards and Tubes, long, weldless .... 6d.
Tiles 1/6
Tinplates .... 5d.
Tinplate Bars .... 4½d.
Trench Covers 1/0
Tubes and Standards, long, weldless .... 6d.
Wire Netting, in Rolls 1/0
Wire, Barbed 1/0
Wool, in Bales .... 7d.
Wire, in Coils .... 4½d.
Wall Shoes .... 6d.
Wire, Old and Cobbles .... 6d.
Wagon and Carriage Work .... 6d.
Wheels and Axles .... 3½d.
Sorting Cargo in Wagons - Double Tariff

Shipping ex Bank from one Crane to another:-
 Extra man or men to be paid the same rate per
 man as the men shipping during the time this
 work is proceeding.

Unloading from Wagons and Warehousing .... 6d.
Shipping from Warehouse .... 6d.
OVERTIME extra .... 2½d.

Shipping Iron and Steel Rails, Sleepers etc.

	No. of Men	Per Ton
Banking Rails	5	4d.
Banking or Shipping Fishplates	4	4½d.
Banking Bowl Sleepers	4	5½d.
Banking Transverse Sleepers	4	5d.

Shipping Iron and Steel Rails, Sleepers etc. - Continued

Banking Bearing Plates by hand	4	4½d.
Shipping Rails	4	4d.
Shipping Transverse Sleepers	4	4½d.
Shipping Bowl Sleepers	4	4½d.
Shipping Scrap Iron	6	6½d.
Shipping Bearing Plates from trucks	4	4d.
Shipping Bearing Plates from bank	4	4½d.
Shipping Railway Accessories in boxes and bags ...	4	4½d.
Loading up Rails by crane	4	3½d.
Loading up Fishplates to trucks by hand	4	5d.

Overtime - One Halfpenny per ton each man extra.

Source: Dock, Wharf, Riverside and General Workers' Union, *Revised Tariff for Discharging, Loading etc., at Docks, Wharves, etc.,* Newport, 1915. The above extract illustrates the variety of general cargoes shipped at the port. Tonnage rates were divided according to the number of dockers in a gang, it was agreed that eight men would handle "foreign" cargoes and six men "coastwise" cargoes.

Appendix 4

THE PORTS AND COALFIELD AREA OF SOUTH WALES

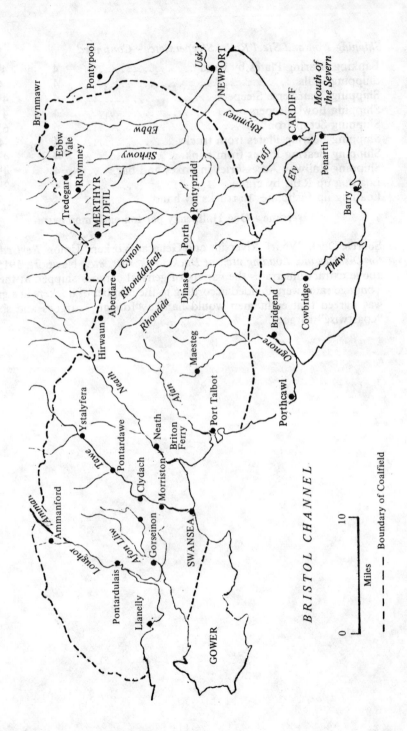

BRISTOL CHANNEL

0   10
Miles

- - - Boundary of Coalfield

Glossary

Although mention is made to the various groups of port workers in the text, a glossary is included for quick reference.

1 Timber Workers

   a Timber Porters. Men employed to receive deals, boards, etc. from the ship and sort and deliver to wagons or piles.

   b Deal runners. Men hired to receive deals from timber porters and stack them in piles.

2 General goods workers. Men employed to receive general goods at the ship's rail, and sort and deliver them to the warehouse.

3 Coal Workers

   a Tippers. Men hired to tip coal into the hold of a vessel by means of hydraulic lifts on the quays called "tips".

   b Coal trimmers. Men employed on board ships to distribute coal evenly in the holds and bunkers.

4 Iron-ore workers. Men employed in the ship's hold to unload iron-ore.

5 Patent fuel workers. Men engaged in the making, conveyance or loading on board ship of patent fuel. Patent fuel was made of a mixture of various kinds of small coals such as steam, anthracite, bituminous coal and pitch. The small coal and pitch were put through a disintegrating machine which ground them to a fine powder. The mixture was conveyed by elevators into large iron cylinders and heated with steam jets until it became plastic. It was filled into moulds by a mechanical arrangement, and pressed with a heavy steam hammer. The bricks were then conveyed to the waterfront.

6 Riggers. Men engaged in fitting ships with wire, rope, tackle and all necessary gear and in attending generally to repairs while the ship was in dock without a crew.

7 Lightermen. Men employed to transport goods in large open boats (lighters) between ships and wharves.

8 Hobblers. In South Wales coal trimmers who were not members of gangs were known as hobblers; but the term also applies to dock pilots who were unlicenced.

9 Boatmen. In the Bristol Channel boatmen were employed to transport cargoes between the various ports; they also moved ships from one wharf to another while the ships were in dock.

Bibliography

In this bibliography I have included the manuscripts, printed records and other materials which have been of most use to me. I am very grateful to the librarians and officials of the libraries and institutions listed below.

Manuscript Sources

Alexandra (Newport and South Wales) Docks and Railway Company, Minute Books, (British Historical Transport Records Office, Royal Oak, London).

Booth Collection (British Library of Political Science, London School of Economics).

Bute Docks Company (renamed Cardiff Railway Company in 1894), Minute Books, 1889-1921, (British Historical Transport Records Office, Royal Oak, London).

Cardiff, Penarth and Barry Coal Trimmers' Protection and Benefit Association, Minute Books, 1888-1921, (University College Library, Swansea).

Webb Trade Union Collection (British Library of Political Science, London School of Economics).

Printed Records

Cardiff Chamber of Commerce, *Annual Reports,* Cardiff, 1891-1914, (Cardiff Central Library).

Cardiff, Penarth and Barry Coal Trimmers' Protection and Benefit Association, *Balance Sheet and Annual Reports,* Cardiff, 1914-18, 1920-1, (British Library of Political Science).

Dock, Wharf, Riverside and General Labourers' (Workers') Union, *Annual Reports,* London, 1889-1921; *Minutes of Annual Delegate Meetings,* London, 1890-6; *Minutes of Triennial Delegate Meetings,* London, 1899, 1902, 1905, 1908, 1914, 1917, 1920, (Transport and General Workers' Union, Transport House, London).

National Amalgamated Labourers' Union of Great Britain and Ireland, *Reports of Branches and General Statement and Summary of Accounts,* Cardiff, 1889-90, 1914, 1918, 1920, (Trades Union Congress; British Library of Political Science).

Parliamentary Papers

Annual Report on Changes in Rates of Wages and Hours of Labour in the United Kingdom, 1894-1901.

Annual Report of Trade Unions by the Chief Labour Correspondent of the Board of Trade, 1890-1913.

Enquiry into the Wages and Conditions of Employment of Dock and Waterside Labourers, 1920.

Report on Strikes and Lock-Outs by the Labour Correspondent to the Board of Trade, 1890-1916.

Royal Commission on Labour, 1892.

Newspapers and Journals

Cambria Daily Leader; Dockers' Record (later renamed *Record); Economic History Review; Economic Journal; Fairplay; Industrial Syndicalist; Industrial World; Justice; Labour Elector; South Wales Argus; South Wales Daily News; South Wales Daily Times and Star of Gwent; South Wales Labour Times; The Times; The Trade Unionist. Welsh Historical Review; Western Daily Press; Workman's Times.*

Books and Pamphlets

Gerald Abrahams, *Trade Unions and the Law,* London, 1968.

V.L. Allen, *Trade Unions and the Government,* London, 1960.

Stan Awbery, *Labour's Early Struggles in Swansea,* Swansea, 1949.

James Bird, *The Major Seaports of the United Kingdom,* London, 1963.

Guy Bowman, *Syndicalism: its Basis, Methods and Ultimate Aim,* London, 1913.

A. Briggs and J. Saville, *Essays in Labour History,* London, 1960.

A. Bullock, *The Life and Times of Ernest Bevin,* London, 1960.

Randolph S. Churchill, *Winston S. Churchill,* London, 1969.

H.A. Clegg, *General Union in a Changing Society,* Oxford, 1964.

H.A. Clegg, A. Fox and A.F. Thompson, *A History of British Trade Unions since 1889,* Oxford, 1964.

M.J. Daunton, *Coal Metropolis: Cardiff 1870-1914,* Leicester, 1977.

E.J. Hobsbawm, *Labouring Men,* London, 1964.

A.H. John, *The Industrial Development of South Wales,* Cardiff, 1950.

E.C.P. Lascelles and S.S. Bullock, *Dock Labour and Decasualisation,* London, 1924.

J. Lovell, *Stevedores and Dockers,* London, 1969.

Tom Mann, *Tom Mann's Memoirs,* London, 1923.

H.A. Mess, *Casual Labour at the Docks,* London, 1916.

W.E. Minchinton, *Industrial South Wales,* London, 1969.

W.E. Minchinton, *The British Tinplate Industry,* Oxford, 1957.

J.A. Morris and L.J. Williams, *The South Wales Coal Industry, 1841-1875,* Cardiff, 1958.

T.J. O'Keefe, *Rise and Progress of the National Amalgamated Labourers' Union of Great Britain and Ireland,* Cardiff, 1891.

Sir David J. Owen, *The Origin and Development of the Ports of the United Kingdom,* London, 1948.

H. Pelling, *A History of British Trade Unionism*, London, 1965.

E.H. Phelps-Brown, *The Growth of British Industrial Relations*, London, 1960.

L.H. Powell, *The Shipping Federation*, London, 1950.

J.K. Price, *The Newport Dock Strike of 1911*, Newport, 1911.

H. Llewellyn Smith and Vaughan Nash, *The Story of the Dockers' Strike*, London, 1889.

P.S. Thomas, *Industrial Relations: A Short Study of the Relations between Employers and Employed in Swansea and Neighbourhood from about 1800 to Recent Times*, Swansea, 1940.

Ben Tillett, *A Brief History of the Dockers' Union*, London, 1910.

Ben Tillett, *Memories and Reflections*, London, 1931.

Dona Torr, *Tom Mann and his Times*, London, 1956.

Edward Tupper, *Seamen's Torch*, London, 1938.

University of Liverpool Department of Social Science, *The Dock Worker*, Liverpool, 1954.

D. Trevor Williams, *The Economic Development of Swansea and of the Swansea District to 1921*, Swansea, 1940.

R. Williams, *The Liverpool Docks Problem*, Liverpool, 1912.

J. Havelock Wilson, *My Stormy Voyage Through Life*, London, 1925.

Theses (Unpublished)

B.J. Atkinson, *The Bristol Labour Movement, 1868-1906*, D. Phil., Oxford, 1970.

D.W. Crowley, *The Origins of the Revolt of the British Labour Movement from Liberalism, 1875-1906*, Ph.D., London, 1952.

H. Hancocks, *History of Tinplate Manufacture in Llanelly*, M.A. Wales, 1965.

G. Phillips, *The National Transport Workers' Federation*, D. Phil., Oxford, 1968.

Index